S-0

P9-BHR-582

6-18-69

THIS DAMNED CAMPUS

as seen by a
college chaplain

ROBERT N.
TAYLOR, JR.

PILGRIM PRESS
Philadelphia
Boston

Copyright © 1969
United Church Press
Philadelphia, Pennsylvania

The scripture quotations in this publication are (unless otherwise indicated) from the *Revised Standard Version of the Bible,* copyrighted 1946 and 1952 by the Division of Christian Education, National Council of Churches, and are used by permission.

The publisher wishes to express appreciation to the individuals and publishers who granted permission to quote their materials. A list of acknowledgments is given on pages 127–30.

Library of Congress Catalog Card No. 77-76086

to
Ruth,
Rick,
Cyndy
for the love
that sustains

C is for Chaplain, a regular guy,
Who's keeping his thumb in that
   pie in the sky.
A liberal Christian fed up
   with hypocrisy,
Disgusted with present-day church
   aristocracy,
A church that's an ark that's
   so messy inside
It can't stay afloat on the
   secular tide;
He preaches reform and rebellions
   galore—
*But I notice he's keeping one foot
in the door!*
      —found on the campus
         Protest Tree
The Ministry is partly being in the
humanities and partly dropping out.
      —Paul Goodman[1]

PREFACE

There is on our campus a live and honorable tradition known as the Protest Tree. Who can tell how much frustration and anger have been relieved by pinning poems and letters on its hoary bark, displaying there a purportedly unpalatable offering of the food service, or hanging in effigy from its branches an occasional administrator?

Once in a while the chaplain's number comes up. The above, written by a many-talented boy now finishing medical studies, beautifully captures the dilemma of today's college chaplain. He is, strange amphibian, a creature of two worlds; one foot in academe, the other in the church. Each of his two worlds may be regarded with suspicion by the other. But while this creates problems, it also provides special opportunities.

Paul Goodman, himself an atheist, has recently written some surprising and perceptive words about the developing role of the campus ministry:

> With dismaying rapidity during the past thirty years, society has become dehumanized. One can tick off the horrors: the Spanish War, World War II, the gas chambers, the atom bomb, the Cold War, the stockpiling

of atom bombs, the Frankenstein-monster technology, the unecological urbanization, the cumbersome centralization, the social engineering, the mass communications, the processing education, the trivializing of democracy. It is in this context that the professions have lost their humane spirit. By contrast the church, so long a pillar of orthodox society, has begun to recall, dimly, that it has something to do with humanity, with persons, with divinity. And young people of intellect and spirit, who cannot breathe in the ambience of dehumanization and factory-education, are often willing to hang around the chaplain. . . . He may be a chump, but he is not a machine and he *might* be serious. . . .

For someone going into the ministry on the basis of these considerations, a campus post makes a lot of sense. It is certainly not an escape from the world, as some touchingly fear, if only because half our population is under twenty-six, forty percent of the college-age group is in college, six million at present; and these students, the dominant inheritors of our social society, are the best hope, finally the sole hope, of altering our doom-bound career.

If a minister means to serve where the need is, this is where the need is.[2]

This book is for all concerned about today's campuses: students, teachers, parents, and others with interest in and regard for the perplexing world of higher education. Let no one be misled by the title, *This Damned Campus*. It is intended simply to suggest that today's campuses have become, for many, a kind of secular equivalent of the churches and synagogues, centers of reflection and struggle within which people make crucial decisions and wrestle with the central agonies and joys of the human condition.

A long time ago, Matthew Arnold referred to Oxford as "the home of lost causes, and forsaken beliefs, and unpopular names, and impossible loyalties." The description is not irrelevant to today's colleges, though those who work there are sustained by the knowledge that some young people emerge from the experience with a sense of purpose and the kind of loyalty which will not easily give way under the pressures of modern life. What the anthropologists call the *rites du passage*, the established rituals by which the young become part of a culture, take place for more and more people today in an academic context. It is here that the young are defining their understanding of themselves, their attitudes toward society, their degree of commitment to something beyond the concerns of the self. But do our colleges tend to reflect too directly the pressures of culture? Is it true, as I have suggested in chapter seven, that men are now justified by "grade," that "making it" and "flunking" have become the contemporary equivalents of salvation and damnation? What can our colleges do to help make the whole experience more genuinely humanizing and liberating?

The progression of the book is easily seen. In the first section, I have tried to function as an interpreter of the bewildering scene to those confused and disturbed by what they have read and heard. If students curious about how a chaplain might "tell it like it is" to outsiders find there some things worth pondering for themselves, I shall not totally have failed my purpose. The second section deals with major personal dilemmas of today's students and grows out of some years of sharing with them their struggles with disillusionment, loneliness, sexual confusion, and academic and cultural pressures. These may be perennial human problems, but I believe they are especially difficult for young people in our changing world. This section also may be useful in helping adults to a more realistic picture of "the hells of ivy." Section III is born of the conviction that, whatever its weaknesses, there is much in the religious tradition that continues to speak powerfully to human need. But if one is to work his way through to a faith-commitment in our world, he must confront, openly, the Freudian critique of religion, the challenge of contemporary philosophers, the perennial problem of evil, and the difficulties of intelligent commitment.

I have written this out of a decade of campus ministry, most of it at Franklin and Marshall College. I am grateful to that college for the freedom to develop the kind of ministry I can affirm and for the constant stimulation, criticism, and challenge

provided by students, faculty, and administrators. The kinds
of problems brought to a college chaplain are bewildering, if
fascinating, in their variety. Clearly no psychiatrist, he is often
confronted with people who are not open to the usual methods
of therapy. Rather "square" himself, he may find himself a
link to one or another campus subculture. Responsible to his
ordination, he may work largely with people who at most are
on the fringes of the religious tradition: indeed many who are
entirely removed, but people who nonetheless hunger for meaning and warmth. Concerned as he must be with the moral dimension of life, he quickly learns that cheap moralism and the
conventional pieties are irrelevant in the face of many of our
current dilemmas.

These essays, then, attempt to shed some light on the complex task of growing up in today's world. They make no claim
to careful scholarship and are born largely of experience. For
their kind interest and many helpful suggestions, I am in-
debted to Prof. Paul Irion of the Lancaster Theological Seminary and Dr. Norman Charles of Millersville State College.
My secretary, Mrs. James Valentine, assisted most generously
in preparing the manuscript.

One of the most profound guides to the dynamics of young
adulthood is Erik Erikson, whose *Young Man Luther* and
Childhood and Society may be read with profit by all who wish
to gain understanding of the intricate processes of human
growth. To him and other writers in the field, to my colleagues
in campus ministry, to those who with patience and wisdom
have sustained me in my own quest, and to those who through
these years have allowed me to share in their search for whole-
ne⌐⌐, I am most grateful.

CONTENTS

part one
WHAT'S GOING ON HERE?

Come, let us go down,
and there confuse their language,
that they may not understand
one another's speech.
 —Genesis 11:7
Teach us to care and not to care.
 —T. S. Eliot[1]
I've got a big investment
in this boy and I expect
a good return on it.
 —a father, overheard
 on Parents' Day
Healthy children will not fear
life if their elders have integrity
enough not to fear death.
 —Erik Erikson[2]
Good fences make good neighbors.
 —Robert Frost[3]
How sharper than a serpent's
 tooth it is
To have a thankless child!
 —William Shakespeare

1
TO
THOSE
OVER
THIRTY

Not long ago, an item appeared in a popular magazine concerning a college financial aid form. Under the heading "Parents' Estimated Worth" was scrawled: "Sentimental Value Only!" Those over thirty may also appreciate the cartoon showing a bedraggled father, walking with his wife from a high school P.T.A. meeting: "Twenty years ago, I was told I wasn't as smart as my father. . . . Today I'm told I'm not as smart as my teen-age boy. . . . Where did we go wrong?"

Where did we go wrong? It's a question asked by most parents from time to time, under the challenging responsibilities of parenthood. Those who can laugh at themselves, on both sides of what is now called the "generation gap," are most able to explore ways in which communication can continue during those difficult years when the necessary quest for autonomy in the young clashes with the necessary parental concern of their elders.

The generational crisis is not new; but that it is intensified in today's Western culture seems obvious. Parents have not gone out of style. The young of all ages still desperately need the stability of their elders and the family, though under siege, becomes increasingly important: an island of personalness in the lonely sea of impersonality. But the conditions of modern life have produced a college generation who from one side of the gap often resemble "spoiled brats," and who, in turn, are frequently persuaded that whatever "authentic" existence may be, they haven't seen much of it at home. Given our rapidly shifting society and the conflicting testimony of the "experts" in human relations, what is really important in promoting and sustaining communication? What are some of the guidelines for navigating the stormy waters of the struggle for independence?

I do not present the following as definitive wisdom. The best I can say for it is that it is first-hand. It emerges largely from ten years of close involvement with both generations across the whole spectrum of concerns: academic grades, money, sexual experimentation, underachievement, unproductive rebellions on the part of students; lack of understanding, emotional immaturity, irrational attitudes, and unproductive attempts to assert authority on the part of parents. That, in addition, I have known students and parents for whom these years have ended in deeper bonds of understanding and love is fortunately quite true. I focus here on problem situations, hoping that others awaiting or now facing the challenge may find something useful.

One thing should be clearly understood. Most colleges today are refusing to act in the place of the parent (*in loco parentis*). Administrators reason that treating students as responsible adults, and allowing them to face the consequences of their own behavior, is an integral part of the educational process. In addition, in today's context, what society legally forbids and what it covertly sanctions are often quite different: though college students under twenty-one are legally forbidden in our state to drink beer, the fraternity beer party is unlikely to be raided so long as things are managed quietly. I am not heartened by the fact that some of our young seem to be making up their own rules as they go; but when they arrive on campus with malleable character structures, there is some question whether strict rule-enforcement is then possible without a restrictive atmosphere harmful to the academic environment.

This is not to excuse the colleges of their responsibilities.

Nor do I believe that most students, despite occasional howls to the contrary, are at all offended by sensible rules which enhance communal life. I suggest that rather than totally disavow the parental task, colleges should be as wise and enlightened "parents" as possible, providing structure and adult presence while encouraging responsible growth toward independence. A reasonable balance of authority and autonomy are needed, though the proper mixture of the two is widely disputed.

What will have happened to today's teen-ager *before* he arrives on campus? Hopefully, he will have a set of values which make sense to him, and which he has sufficient strength to affirm. Hopefully, he will have learned to avoid the unnecessary dangers accompanying the growing-up process and will have made positive and healthful social attachments which make unproductive rebellions quite unnecessary. How? Who, finally, really knows? But it has long seemed to me that the best parents are those who manage, somehow, to avoid the twin pitfalls of tyranny and abdication, of overcaring and undercaring. There are those who appear to care too much and those who appear to care too little.

What of the relatively uncaring? Don't tune out at this point. I am aware that none of us will admit that we don't really care about our young. The idea! But, somehow, a number of today's young people have got that distinct impression. Some of them seem to be crying out (often in devious ways) for rules, for guidance. When a boy tells me of his resentment of his parents, and can only come up with "They're always too damned nice to me" for an explanation, he is telling all of us that virtual lack of structure is just as bad as the authoritarianism of another day.

Going through my counseling notes of some years, I have noticed that many students who lack motivation, are apathetic and underachieving, have in common a problem at home which I can best describe as "the absent father," absent not alone in the physical but also in the emotional sense. Those students who are very confused about values, who get in continual trouble, who annoy faculty with their apparently stubborn refusal to take hold—frequently those young men are from upper-middle-class homes, that very segment of our society where one finds fathers deeply involved in the rat race. Those young with the joyless rebellions, those rebels without a cause . . . have their fathers really been "there" for them? Has there been any steady discipline in the context of warmth? Have there been consistent and sensible rules? Have these young men had a solid and visible force with which to identify, and against which to forge out their own growing convictions?

This is not to discount the pressures on a great many men in their personal and vocational struggles in our day. Few of us escape them. Nonetheless there is evidence that it is the harried father, who has little time or enthusiasm for his children, who is most likely to be troubled later on by a son who can't make commitments: to a job, a girl, a way of life. All of us must struggle with the identity problem on our way to adulthood; the boy in question is disadvantaged, chiefly because one can't identify with what is not really there. Contemporary literature provides us with a number of illustrations of this problem, the most notable being that of Willy Loman in Arthur Miller's *Death of a Salesman*. Unwilling to face his own weakness, unwilling to disavow a phony and hopeless dream of success, bounding in and out of his home between business trips, Willy winds up with boys who can't grow up, hold jobs, make intelligent plans. It isn't at all surprising that today's students hunger for positive and forceful leaders; and if the ones they select may occasionally seem to us shrill and themselves immature, we need to ask ourselves if we have given them an adequate model of a man.

I have recently come across two studies which lend weight to the "absent father" observation. One, psychiatrist Seymour L. Halleck's "Alienation of Students," concludes: "The future alienated person does not experience his father as a strong person. More likely, he has spent most of his early life in the company of his mother and knows his father as a likeable, but shadowy, figure." The other, by Donald Barr ("What Did We Do Wrong?") appeared in *The New York Times Magazine* of November 26, 1967. Suggesting that many of today's American adolescents are deficient in superego (conscience, internalized social controls), Mr. Barr charges that today's parents have

JOHN BENSON

frequently failed to transmit moral and intellectual values to their children. "The incontinent giving of things, the promiscuous giving of permission, and the weak withholding of imperatives are all equivalent. They amount to the denial of denial, a cruel trick to play on children and on adolescents."

Mr. Barr also traces to overpermissiveness (emptiness?) some other things noticed on today's campuses: the lack of a perception of time ("the now generation"); the inability to work for future goals; aggressive behavior between the sexes (the "gross out"), probably related to frustration at having no sense of purpose; and the questionable turning of attention from the problems of the external world to what's happening inside one's head.

The underachieving student is most perplexing. The key question is: Whom is he punishing? As suggested above, a student may be taking revenge on his parents, without being aware of it, for failing to control him and teach him the necessity of effort. Again, the student may be reacting to what he perceives as overcontrol; there are some parents who appear to care too much, "appear," since the caring may well be related to their own neurotic needs.

And if the abdicators, the undercaring, cause problems, is it not obvious that there is such a thing as unwarranted interference? To refer once more to the underachiever, is it at all surprising that the student who feels he's been pushed into a course of study will resent it? When a girl feels she's been programmed all her life to fit her mother's dream, how will she react? Or when a father's frantic insistence on his son's "success" measures, not his love for his son, but his own thwarted desire for prestige—how fares the son?

Detective-story writer Dorothy Sayers, marvelous theologian that she also was, describes in *The Mind of the Maker* the parallels between an artist's proper love for his creation and a parent's proper love for his child. Of that love she writes:

> Two popular interpretations of the word we can dismiss at once: the creator's love for his work is not a greedy possessiveness; he never desires to subdue his work to himself but always to subdue himself to his work. The more genu-

inely creative he is, the more he will want his work to develop in accordance with its own nature, and to stand independent of himself.

And if creative love is not possessive, neither is it sentimental. Writers have, admittedly, been sentimental over their creatures from time to time, but never without the loss of creative power. . . .

The sentimentality that distorted their [characters'] true natures to give them an artificial happiness was no act of creative love.

"Sacrifice" is another word liable to misunderstanding. It is generally held to be noble and loving in proportion as its sacrificial nature is consciously felt by the person who is sacrificing himself. The direct contrary is the truth. To feel sacrifice consciously as self-sacrifice argues a failure in love.[4]

Wise words, these, when pondered and applied to parental responsibilities. Quite likely, the best thing one can do to assure his child of a relatively smooth path to maturity is to be a reasonably happy and productive human being oneself. Parents with persisting troubles ought not to avoid getting help. If one is relatively comfortable emotionally, isn't there much less chance that he'll mess things up by trying to live, vicariously, through his son or daughter? One recalls Carl Jung's observation that the greatest influence on the child is "the unlived life of the parent."

Parents are quite right in continuing to be concerned about students' values and moral decisions while in college. If they are not, who, in any careful way, will be? We should not, out of some false sophistication, forget the importance of the peer group. Though it may sound like an old Sunday school bromide, that warning about "the company you keep" remains sound. Parents also have a right to be concerned about the atmosphere and quality of dormitory life. And before we are too glib in urging teens to "stand on their own two feet," we need remember that approval from others his age is a young person's lifeblood. Parents can show that they understand this. They, too, need the approval of their friends, and they ought not hesitate to explain that this is one of the reasons why such things as trimmed hair and decorum do matter to them; "what the neighbors think" affects them just as "what the kids think" affects the child. Communication is a two-way street.

It is also important to be realistic about grades. Parents have both a right and an obligation to expect reasonable work and discipline. They must not expect the impossible. They must reckon with the stiffness of competition in today's colleges. It is indeed harder than it was thirty years ago, a fact which alumni verbalize but find hard to accept. Unrealistic pressure is more likely to make that "C" an "F" than an "A."

Abraham of old was commanded to take the life of his son as a test of his loyalty to God. This story has often been an offense to moderns, but how often have we observed parents sacrificing their own children on the altars of personal discontent or social pressure! The case of the Arizona coed, who chose suicide as an alternative to shooting the pet she loved most, may be soberly pondered by all who regard themselves as reasonable. People who allow their children no acceptable options ought not be surprised if irrational behavior follows. Nobody who has lived in a dormitory will forget how shattering a nagging phone call from home can be. Steady "flak" breeds hopelessness. Hot tongue and cold shoulder do not nourish academic performance.

Given a true attempt on the part of students to perform with credit, we must somehow learn to support them in occasional and inevitable failures. In fact, shouldn't we be teaching them, from our own experience, that the ability to withstand painful defeat is one of life's essential ingredients? Let's show steady concern, but be sure that such concern is not a subtle weapon with which to control.

With respect to social behavior, there is, as I have suggested, an almost dizzying freedom on many of today's campuses, and changing moral standards do not make less troublesome the predictable human tragedies which follow suit. One can only hope that responsible attitudes and a concern for others have been built into the student during the precollege years. One hopes that the lines of communication will remain open and that, if parents don't totally approve of everything that's going on, they will at least be *aware* of what's going on!

Finally, again, we ought to keep things in perspective. Being a parent involves much more than a worrisome responsibility, and I have not intended to discuss the matter as some clergymen continue to discuss sex: as though it were largely a somber and disturbing thing. So far, I've much enjoyed being "Daddy," though my licks may be coming! In any event, it does seem important to accentuate the positive and recall that most of us have, somehow, muddled our way into something resembling maturity in spite of our all-too-human parents. Maybe there's hope for all of us.

This college has nothing
to teach me.
　　　—a student
Religion that is pure and undefiled
before God ... is this ... to keep
oneself unstained from the world.
　　　—James 1:27
Weep not, dear reader, for youth's
neglected majority: business and
law firms care for their own.
　　　—John Kretzmann
When reviled, we bless;
when persecuted, we endure ... ;
we have become, and are now,
as the refuse of the world,
the offscouring of all things.
　　　—1 Corinthians 4:12b–13b
Why do I wear a beard?
It locates my friends and
it keeps away the others.
　　　—a student
In the fifties, some sought
security at the expense of identity
and became organization men, others
sought identity at the expense of
security and became beatniks.
　　　—Arthur Schlesinger

2
HIP,
HIP,
HOORAY?

To outsiders, who must depend mainly on the mass media or hearsay, today's campuses must appear bizarre. Indeed, a prominent California educator, Dr. Max Rafferty, used as part of a successful campaign speech for nomination as United States Senator the contention that an education at Berkeley was a "four-year course in sex, drugs, and treason." Such generalizations ought not to merit much respect, even less when applied to the whole spectrum of American higher education, but Americans (while their billboards staunchly reassure them that "College Is America's Best Friend") are concerned.

A standard response of college administrators to attacks on student extremists is the accurate reminder that the students (and non-students) who make the headlines are a small minority. But extremist positions often reflect widespread moods and attitudes. And if relatively few of the young are "hippies" (the passive phase of student discontent) or militant rebels (the active phase), one finds a widespread sympathy and fascination with both groups among many of today's students and a resentment of adults who too easily "put them down."

Alienation is a word so variously applied that I almost hesitate to use it. But, for all its vagueness, it points to something very characteristic of our time. Students for some years have been fascinated with Albert Camus' *The Stranger,* the portrayal of a man with what a psychiatrist might call "flattened affect," a man disengaged emotionally from the usual attachments and responsibilities of society. What we are seeing on today's campuses is an apparently growing number of young people who are giving up on the usual goals of academic and social life, who are rebelling only in the most passive sense by "dropping out" and by substituting for concern with what the rest of us call reality an intense preoccupation with the inner workings of their own minds.

Each daily newspaper documents the phenomenon: black militants simply don't care what white people want or think; a student leaves for Canada because a questionable war in Southeast Asia seems no reason for him to risk death; a brilliant college senior refuses his diploma and "hits the road"; the use of marijuana appears with increasing regularity in suburban high schools; and, in diverse ways throughout the country, the young are informing the world that they no longer find meaning in American society and have discovered, sometimes through mind-expanding drugs, deeper levels of meaning than the rest of us know. What's going on here?

Having been quite close to one corner of the scene for some years, I suggest that we resist the almost overwhelming temptation to dismiss such phenomena as the ravings of a bunch of "kooks, quacks, and perverts." This gesture is a useful adult tranquilizer, but it suffers from the defect of being untrue. To concentrate only on the hippies and to conclude, reassuringly, that they are after all a decided minority—this is to miss the point. A recent survey conducted by the editors of *Look* of undergraduate newspaper editors merely confirmed what some of us see at first hand: Alienation is not confined to any lunatic fringe. Its influence is powerful even among the most apparently conventional of today's students. And the key thing about the publicized minority of today's students is that, in many ways, they set the tone and ethos for the larger group— and if you don't believe me, check what's considered "in" at your local high school.

The film *The Graduate* baffled (and angered) a good

many people; students on our campus were singing its praises long before it appeared in this area. With what in Benjamin do they identify? His feeling that adults are continually pressuring him to "do" something? His inability to be thrilled by a career in plastics? His reaction to his parents' obtuseness, as well as to the gaudy affluence and distorted values of his elders, including neurotic if seductive Mrs. Robinson? Something obviously hit a vital spot.

But if we must face this issue, we need not exaggerate it to the point of distortion. Let's not be overawed by the generation gap. The overawed adult simply makes the possibilities of a "put-on" more appealing. One essential ingredient, surely, in looking at some of these problems, is a sense of humor. Somewhere, Søren Kierkegaard speaks of humor as the ability to see the world's problems while continuing to love. Students, in the tradition of Goethe's young Werther, often take themselves far too seriously, and parents who respond in kind simply complicate the issue. There is an important sense, indeed, in which the young depend on us *not* to take them too seriously!

Another thing parents ought to remember is quite simple: These *are*, after all, your children. They have not suddenly bloomed forth *de novo*. Many of the attitudes the young now hold to extremes that frighten adults are not totally foreign to those with functioning memories. The preoccupations of youth are rooted in their backgrounds. A classic example of this was provided some years ago on television's "The Life of Riley." Riley is worried about daughter and boyfriend downstairs in the living room. Peg tries to comfort him: "Chester, remember how it was when you were young?" Riley screams: "I'll moider da bum!" After all, if we take credit for the admirable kids who serve impressively in VISTA and the Peace Corps, who take part responsibly in civil rights and peace activities, who work seriously at their studies and professional training, we must also take credit for the rest. The current phenomena are not part of a Communist plot; they are explainable in terms of the inner logic of our culture.

One perplexing example: drugs. Parents are horrified to read of college students' experimentation. But look around you. Are there psychedelic shops in your community? How much money has been made by psychedelic themes and artwork in the records and magazines? Why did my sixth-grader report that kids in his class were wearing beads and sandals, joking about sugar cubes? And isn't it so that the United States is the most drug-consuming, drug-oriented society in human history? Haven't our children been exposed, since birth, to that electronic baby-sitter which continually assures us that all of our problems will be cured by putting a magic substance under our arms or in our mouths? We are a turned-on culture! Perhaps we should face this first, then raise the question about campus drug experimentation.

Let me be quite clear: there is very real danger in such experimentation. But there is also a real need for parents and others to apply their intelligence to what has been made to appear a totally mysterious and somehow sinister area of life. I am not an expert in this area, but I've been privileged to attend some conferences on drugs and have listened to many of the experts. Let me say, briefly, that there are three drugs which appear most frequently on today's campuses. Of the three, L.S.D. (and related psychedelics) seems to appear least, if only because there are obvious risks and some indication that chromosomal damage may result. The amphetamines ("speed") are apparently more widespread. Some of you will recall how widely they were used in weight-control by physicians only a few years ago. These are risky and can, in certain people, be addictive. They are dangerous emotionally and physically.

The most perplexing problem for college administrators concerns marijuana ("mary jane," "pot," "tea," "grass"). Shall they evict anyone suspected of smoking or caught using it? Shall they, indeed, expel some of their brightest students? What can one say? Many have noticed a correlation between marijuana smoking and academic failure, though no causal relationship can yet be demonstrated. Marijuana, like alcohol, may be used by people already in trouble as a way of avoiding the pain. There is some evidence that pot leads to a kind of psychological dependence (what you like you tend to repeat), but there is no evidence at all that it is addictive or that it necessarily leads to using something more potent. And somehow the risk of "psychological dependence" does not seem persuasive to a generation who have grown up noting adult dependence on everything from aspirin to alcohol. Even Dr. Goddard of the Food and Drug Administration recently admitted that, faced with the choice, he'd rather have his daughter use marijuana than liquor. Needless to say, that brewed plenty of hot water.

So what, finally, can be said? This: that however uncertain we are at present as to the long-range medical and psychological effects of marijuana, we *are* certain of its social consequences. Presently its use may lead to a lengthy jail term and a career-hampering felony on one's record. Is it worth that? And this: that we need the young to help us change the world, and those whose lives center around subjective experiences, and who respond mainly to their own internal circuits, are not likely to be of much use; that mental masturbation is as immature psychologically as prolonged autoeroticism is sexually; that those who feel the need of chemical support are better advised to get expert help; that life itself should be a sufficiently good trip at age twenty, and, if it's not, the reasons can with profit be examined.

But again, if we are to help, we need perspective and intelligent discernment. One father reported to me, shocked, that he had found "dope" taped under the family jalopy. What did he mean by "dope"? "Things like heroin and marijuana." I tried to make the distinction which is easily blurred over in our culture. I further asked him whether he, himself, ever used drugs? "No!" "Alcohol?" "Well . . . " "Tranquilizers?" "Well . . ."

I have concentrated on the drug problem only because it mightily concerns parents and because it is symptomatic of the overall problem, alienation, that here concerns us. A decade ago, in *Growing Up Absurd*, Paul Goodman presented a disturbing preview of things to come. Warning that it was becoming impossible for the bright and sensitive young to find meaning in our increasingly technological world, with its impersonality and questionable values, Goodman delineated the alienated of the fifties: the cynical, the "beat," the resigned, the delinquent. In May of 1967, the Franklin and Marshall College Health Services issued a significant report detailing trends in the nature and frequency of problems brought to college counselors. Noting that in four years some dramatic changes had taken place, the report began by suggesting possible causes: increased pressure and competition, consequent loss of self-esteem, the draft (which tends to make college performance a matter of life or death), and "a progressively deteriorating respect for authority." Noting a pervasive· rejection of society's right to impose "rules" in such matters as the use of alcohol and sexual behavior, the report suggested that rational authority and meaningful laws remain necessary in any social structure. It then listed two noticeable shifts:

> By far the most significant increase in our problems seems to be in the areas of apathy, indifference, lack of motivation, and essentially giving up the fight. Many students complain of inability to go on, to get out of bed, to get to class, to write papers and do assignments even though they are aware of the potential consequences. What is disheartening is that many of these people were formerly good students. We suspect that this reaction is largely due to anger and frustration about the ceaseless pressure felt and doubts about one's ability to meet the myriad expectations of others. A large number of such students have said that they would leave college for a year or longer if it were not for the draft. In counseling, evidence of resentment is powerful, since students feel they no longer have any free choice as to what to do with their lives.

> Another pattern increasingly seen involves the student who openly or tacitly admits that he has been taking drugs (marijuana, L.S.D., barbiturates and amphetamines) and who shows great indifference to the potential consequences. Several characteristics are common in this group. In the first instance they are students who have long been alienated from the mainstream of their peers for a variety of reasons. They have a mixed bag of problems, but in common is a conviction that the society as it is now constituted cannot offer them what they need. They generally, however, cannot define very precisely what it is they do need. They tend to be an intellectually competent if not superior group who have both given up the battle

and said it is not worth it. Typically, they are loners who have found others with whom they feel a tenuous comradeship. They tend to feel that communal drug use facilitates feelings of closeness which are otherwise beyond their grasp.

This report confirms my own observations and closely parallels other independent studies. Helen B. Shaffer's "Alienated Youth," Kenneth Kenniston's *The Uncommitted*, Seymour Halleck's study of alienated students, and a whole host of popular-magazine interviews with students themselves beat out the litany: pressure, loneliness, affluence, phony values, Vietnam, the new technology, depersonalization, the new interest in religion, experimentation with sex and drugs.

So much for the students. What about the rest of us? Is there anything we need to learn? I was much intrigued by *Harper's* recent "Dialogue Between the Generations." Walter Lippmann (who is wiser?) noted that the older generation did have one thing to contribute: wisdom, the capacity to make sound judgments. Rita Dershowitz replied:

> The wisdom that may or may not be on the other side of the generation gap simply isn't relevant to my life.
>
> I deeply feel the inadequacy of the values I learned while growing up. Categories of social worth; drive for possession of things and people; the academic definitions of what is worth knowing and doing; the myth of America's good intentions around the world—all of these break down in the search for what is really important, and for a style of life that has dignity.[1]

I suggest we listen, with some seriousness, to the indictments of "society" which leap at us from every newspaper and journal; they are legion. Consider, as just one example, "The Tragedy of Thomas Dodd" as reported by one of the Senator's former aides, about the investigation of the television industry. Despite convincing evidence that the steady diet of crime, inane romance, and senseless violence which screams at us from "the tube" has been deliberately designed by a few executives to up ratings and income, nothing has been done. In the face of sober opinions by psychologists of the brutalizing effect of such a steady diet, adult moralizing about youthful sex experimentation and "crime in the streets" takes on a hollow sound. Just who *is* God in our society?

And as for the world scene:

> Linus (to Lucy): "Charlie Brown says that brothers and sisters can learn to get along. . .
>
> "He says they can get along the same way mature adults get along. . .
>
> "And he says that adults can get along the same way that nations get along. . ."
>
> (pause)
>
> "At this point the analogy breaks down."[2]

There is the story of a New York stockbroker who said to his son, "Things were tense the other day on the market. We had a peace threat." Suicide attempts by returning soldiers from Vietnam add another grim dimension and serve to remind us that Allan Ginsberg's "Howl" and Bob Dylan's "Masters of War" are not merely the ravings of the deranged.

A fascinating kind of communication took place, I think, at one of our college's Sunday luncheons. We bring to campus a steady parade of people who speak directly to the problems of today's young as they understand them. This particular Sunday we had an unexpected "happening." I had suggested that our visitor, an elderly and respected psychiatrist from New York City, talk about "The Hippies' Quest for Reality." The people at the luncheons were living illustrations of the "gap": college faculty and administrators, local psychologists and psychiatrists, a contingent of about a dozen "hippies," a number of clergymen and seminary professors, and some people from the community who came out of personal interest.

Announcing that years ago he had been a human "guinea pig" in an experiment with mescaline, and reporting the feelings of "reality" in the experience, Dr. Gotthard Booth immediately caught the attention of all. After noting the real dangers in all drug experimentation and recommending extreme caution, he went on to describe the fascination with "mind-expanding" substances as symptomatic of a profound absence in our culture of spiritual depth and peace.

> The hippie movement is a meaningful revolt against the extremes of materialism and depersonalization in our technological civilization. The present form of the revolt cannot become a viable form of human existence, but neither can humanity survive if it continues to develop into the means by which machines multiply, as Norbert Wiener put it. The revolt seems to have stirred up some greater awareness in many that there is more to life than material welfare.[3]

Dr. Booth served as a kind of catalyst. His speech was almost a verbal Rohrschach test. Everybody's presuppositions, fears, and fascinations emerged, from one young man's testimonial ("I wish I could turn you all on!") to psychiatrists' worry about the pathological qualities in mystical and psychedelic experiences. Dr. Booth concluded, forcefully, by urging a nonchemical approach to the quest for inward serenity, affirming that by prayer or "transcendental meditation," the discipline of the spirit, Western man can discover for himself that peace and meaning for which he strives. All present were taken seriously. They were listened to, they had a chance to speak without fear, and, I think, all did some listening too.

After all, isn't this the important thing? There will always be a kind of gulf between generations, indeed, the gulf is probably a psychological blessing, but it can issue either in creative differences or in ruinous failure of communication. To be able to listen, to seek to understand, to share with one another our deepest yearnings, problems, and feelings . . . is this not to be human in the deepest sense? We owe it to the young not to be overwhelmed by them. We must hold forth to them structures, convictions, a solid force against which they can push. We also owe it to them to see that the lines are open at our end. Alienation is not a necessary response to today's world. But increasing communication is a necessary prelude to a better tomorrow.

O matter and impertinency mix'd.
Reason in madness.
　　　—William Shakespeare
Fervent patriotism as well as
religious and revolutionary
enthusiasm often serves as a refuge
from a guilty conscience.
　　　—Eric Hoffer
I am comfortable with interracial
social situations, casual use of
marijuana and the mind-expanding
drugs...
　　　—Rita Dershowitz[1]
What this country needs is
radicals who will stay that way—
regardless of the creeping years,
the inevitable blunders, defeats,
and combat fatigue.
　　　—John Fischer
Do not be conformed to this
world...
　　　—Paul, Romans 12:2a
Let every person be subject to
the governing authorities.... He who
resists the authorities resists
what God has appointed...
　　　—Paul, Romans 13:1a–2a

3
THE
CAMPUS
REBELS

If alienation is a puzzling and disturbing thing, more recent months have seen an increase in campus activities no less calculated to raise the blood pressures and anxieties of administrators, parents, and other observers of the collegiate scene. Even following the disturbances at Berkeley in 1965, few were prepared for the massive revolt at Columbia University in the spring of 1968 or for similar occurrences on all sorts of campuses throughout the country. And since we have been accustomed to student uprisings in *other* countries for years, it was not much comfort that President DeGaulle, too, had his hands full. And if Hayakawa can't communicate—who can?

There is a nice touch of irony in all this. In the late forties and fifties, when I was in college and seminary, educational pundits got a lot of after-dinner mileage bemoaning the apolitical, apathetic stance of their "bank clerk" students toward the problems of society. We were denounced as the "silent generation," the "bland leading the bland," the unfortunate educational by-products of the "Eisenhower years." College administrators today, be assured, have consigned that speech to the circular file. The clever turn of phrase "Rebel, ye dispersers" has become again "Disperse, ye rebels!"

What goes on? Have the kids gone mad? Have administrators lost the capacity to administer? What about the faculty? Just who's in charge here? Elsewhere in this book, I intend to deal with specific problems and decisions facing today's students. Here, as self-styled interpreter to the over-thirty set, let me make what I hope will be some useful observations about what Robert MacAfee Brown has called "those revolting students."

First, understanding will be served if we avoid the popular tendency to substitute slogans for discussion of issues. Articles on student discontent which pontificate about the generation gap or "the Berkeley syndrome" are, for the most part, tedious and unproductive. Of course there is a perennial clash between the young and the not so young, but there is also a sense in which each generation is a group of evolving variables. We ought not to depersonalize today's young by lumping them all in a "generation" anymore than they ought to do the same to their elders by assuming that all past thirty are equally benighted. As students are quick to comment, the real issues are not age and generation; they are white racism, American power and responsibility, poverty in an affluent society, impersonality, and needed reforms in education. Let's avoid smokescreens of rationalization. And even if we take it as a matter of course that, among today's campus rebels, some appear to be acting out patterns of emotional disturbance and others seem interested in "fun and games," these evidences of human frailty should not for a moment be allowed to obscure the real problem: Rightly or wrongly, a disturbing number of today's college students are convinced that things are seriously amiss in these United States and that, furthermore, radical and forceful means are necessary to remedy the matter. This applies not only to society in general but to the colleges as microcosms of that society. And it is a problem which expands to include all of us, as we question our effectiveness as individuals in shaping our own destiny and that of institutions to which we give our allegiance. As perceptive a commentator as David Brinkley mentioned, on the eve of the 1968 Republican National Convention, his growing frustration over the fact that those who controlled the political processes in his state (Maryland) seemed both impervious to and unconcerned about the wishes of many of the electorate. Is this sense at the core of the "new politics"?

Later, I intend to suggest a central cause for the *intensity* of disenchantment among today's students. Now, without minimizing in any way the very real problems which concern them, let me suggest a number of things about the current college generation which may help us set immediate points in a broader context.

To begin with, there are so many of them. The sheer variety and number of students today is surely one reason for the growing importance of their opinions and attitudes. And they have money! Hence, they are courted, publicized, and frequently presumptuous to an unusual degree. If some of them seem more than ordinarily arrogant, if they often need George Bernard Shaw's reminder that no man is infallible, not even a young one, we ought to ask ourselves to what extent this tendency to take themselves too seriously is a function of a dominant trend in our culture.

> We are in danger of becoming obsessed by the young; in our lives, in our thinking, in our politics. . . . We should be careful not to spoil the young by a false, and condescending, obsequiousness or flattery. We should not, by taking them too seriously, invite them too early to take themselves too seriously as well. . . .
>
> From the flat and decent plateau of middle age, we can envy them many of their opportunities, material and immaterial. But what one cannot envy them is the syrup of "understanding" in which their elders seem determined to drown them.[2]

Today's collegians are growing to maturity at a time when our whole society is expanding its notion of individual freedom. Their parents, themselves often college-educated and liberal, began some of the very social revolutions they now dismiss. With the recent Supreme Court decisions, it is probably fair to say that, politically, individuals in our society have been accorded more liberties than in any other. But, at the same time, many people *feel* less free. As Richard Rovere has bril-

MAURY ENGLANDER

liantly informed us (in "Freedom: Who Needs It?"), while we are accorded great personal and political liberty, massive social forces generate the sense of powerlessness; it is a sad fact of life that individual voices of disagreement in a mass society like ours often go unheeded. So students, who from their parents' point of view have more liberties than are possibly good for them, may nonetheless genuinely feel that their colleges and universities make of them little more than impersonal statistics, appendages to their ID cards.

I would not argue that today's students are the brightest in human history, but they are certainly more aware of their world, and for the same reason that many of their elders have also become so: the intrusive and inescapable presence of the mass media. The twenty-one-inch tube has an astonishing influence. It is helpful to recall that assassinations of national leaders have recently thrown people into clinical depressions, even caused suicides; that it is next to impossible to accept, let alone ignore, a war which erupts nightly into your living room or dormitory lounge on the Huntley-Brinkley show; that there is a kind of dangerous excitement, sloganizing, even demagoguery surrounding many of our current political discussions. This is an electronically turned-on culture, with or without benefit of Marshall McLuhan!

Whatever psychological deprivations today's young have suffered, it is true that many college students have had, materially, pretty much what they've needed. I do not presume to speak for black students, whose context and self-understanding are quite different. But most American college students have not known "hot" wars or economic depressions; nor, one suspects, have they ever had to struggle much for anything. I do not make too much of this, but simply suggest that there is what a psychologist might call "low frustration tolerance" among many of today's young; hence losing a girl, failing a course, discovering that one's political convictions (no matter how intensely held) do not immediately or inevitably translate themselves into public policy—all these can be bitter pills to swallow. And the frustration is intensified when public officials continue to parrot a rhetoric once believable, but no longer seriously entertained in college or high school classrooms. High school teachers have taught students to make more careful distinctions than those of J. Edgar Hoover ("godless communism," "juvenile delinquency"); they see through many things which were sufficiently convincing to the young of previous generations. Often, therefore, our institutions (governments, churches, corporations) simply do not command their respect. They feel strongly that they have been lied to, deceived, and a favorite campus expression, accompanied by a look of incredulity and a tale about the latest official explanation, tells the story well: "I don't believe it!"

Yet haven't governments always lied to their people? And what about the lies in television commercials? Don't the alleged hypocrisies of adults, as Kenneth Keniston has suggested, reflect the fact that adults in our culture are themselves caught in a conflict between the value structures of their childhood and their adult perceptions? And isn't it so that power politics is still a grim reality, even if one doesn't choose Mr. Hoover as one's political analyst?

"Of course," to all these questions. But we have somehow failed to convey to many of today's students the other side of the story, an awareness of the complexity of life and its problems, of the perennial and stubborn nature of evil in human and social experience. We have, I think, failed them educationally. In fact, this seems to me the *core* of today's mood of disenchantment and rebellion. It is not that the young are wrong in their recognition of the abiding problems of American life; it is rather that today's students have, if anything, been "oversold" on the possibility of reform, as if, having literally believed that their world could be remade quickly and thoroughly, they now bitterly reject a society which appears to them to resist perversely their ideals, their efforts, their dreams, their rhetoric, their demonstrations.

Why should this be so? Partly because today's students started thinking seriously about life about the time of John Fitzgerald Kennedy's election and the "New Frontier." Who of Kennedy's admirers will forget the heady wine of hope, the growing conviction that this sordid globe might yet be "remade, nearer to the heart's desire"? Who will forget the early and exciting days of civil rights, the "discovery" of poverty (the poor already knew about it), the nuclear test ban treaty, the graceful intelligence and culture of the White House family? Even after Kennedy's tragic assassination, the mood continued. Theologian William Hamilton (in a now-famous essay called "The New Optimism: From Prufrock to Ringo") commented that the Beatles, in their life-affirming naturalness, had replaced the gloomy, introspective characters of T. S. Eliot; he saw great significance in the fact that Eliot died on the night Lyndon Johnson announced the launching of the Great Society.

I need not remind any reading this book how strange all this seems from the perspective of recent months. Enthusiasm for civil rights and the goal of integration has, for the moment, been replaced by the intricacies of "black power" and fear of riots. Within a few years, our involvement in the affairs of a tiny nation in Southeast Asia has changed the mood of an entire world. And all those government programs on behalf of the poor—some have, in fact, been tremendously productive, but the country is not in an affirming mood. Exit Camelot. Enter same, grubby old world. And with it a mood of disappointment and disenchantment. However frustrating the protracted war in Vietnam, however naturally odious the thought of interrupting one's education and fighting for a cause one finds it hard to affirm, there is as much keenness as wit in this comment by Prof. Richard Schier of the Franklin and Marshall department of government: "It is true that interest in the political process has risen markedly on college campuses in recent months, following upon the discovery that the foreign policy of a great nation does not yield readily to tactics appropriate for desegregating a hot dog stand."

What we have somehow failed to convey to students today is the plain recognition that many of the world's problems are exceedingly complex; that there are situations in which, for the moment, little that is helpful can be done; that, in short, there may be something about human nature itself which will forever defy Utopia—that this insight does not in itself mean that we are "selling out." Some adults, of course, do sell out. But there is no reason whatever why young and old can't plan and work *together* to do what they can to make this world a somewhat better place. And if that sort of suggestion does not bring forth a chorus of cheers, it may nonetheless be a reasonable one.

It is sobering to ask how much of the current disaffection of the young is due to the commendable aims of clergymen, college professors, and others who, in their wish to inspire in their young friends social concern and enthusiasm, may have given them a very incomplete picture of their world. The going "religion" of contemporary academe, secular humanism, is particularly apt to oversell the young on the innate goodness and power of men along with the accompanying suspicion that the real source of evil lies in social institutions and traditions. Philosophers of all ages have generally known better.

> The first object of a political education is to dispel in the citizen's mind the manifold utopian notions of man's nature and of the nature of the world with which he emerges from the arduous experience of adolescence. He has to learn that men are moved not only by principle but by interest, that their actions are aimed not only at the discharge of duty but also at the satisfaction of passion, appetite, and unreflecting habit. He has to learn that the world in which he acts is a world of scarcity and that all the resources at his disposal are limited, both material resources of wealth and immaterial ones of time and political support. He must learn that all these resources have alternative uses between which he must choose, and that generally his choice is irrevocable.[3]

Here is an insight as old as biblical realism, as familiar as the observation of Sir Thomas More:

> If evil persons cannot be quite rooted out, and if you cannot correct habitual attitudes as you wish, you must not therefore abandon the commonwealth. You must strive to guide policy indirectly, so that you can make the best of things, and what you cannot turn to good, you can at least make less bad. For *it is* impossible to do all things well unless all men are good, and this I do not expect to see for a long time.

Students are correct, of course, in observing that such "realism" is frequently used as a tranquilizer and apparent antidote against the need for action. But realism need not preclude effective action (indeed it is the ineffectiveness of much campus rebellion that troubles some of us most), as witness the remarkable career of Reinhold Niebuhr. Niebuhr's life continues to teach us how a stern and historically grounded assessment of human limitations can go hand in hand with passionate and effective involvement in politics. What we have failed to teach many students is beautifully expressed by the French writer Alain: "One must stand firm between two kinds of madness, that of believing that one can do anything, and that of believing one can do nothing." What we need to say and demonstrate, again and again, is that there are some things we can do that are worth doing, even though there are others which will forever resist our best hopes and efforts. The process of coming to terms with this fact has been known, traditionally, as growing up.

Part of the glory of being young, of course, is that one does not find such distinctions very appealing. The young like things clear-cut, decisive, dramatic. But I am happy to report that few students with whom I've talked would have much respect for the complaint of this Berkeley senior: "The trouble with trying to understand politics and society as they are taught in the university is that everything seems so complex, so subject to a multitude of seemingly unrelated or contradictory constructions and interpretations." (Quoted by Gerald Rosenfeld in "Generational Revolt and the Free Speech Movement.")

Most of the disenchanted students are not, I think, that naïve. Nor do they all disavow the political process. But that we have been having a "crisis of confidence" in this country in the past several years is clear, and the events of 1968 have only served to dramatize that crisis. The assassination of Robert F. Kennedy, with his special appeal to the young, the poor, the black, was a harsh blow to all. It is true that the campaign of Senator Eugene McCarthy showed that today's students will work enthusiastically in politics for candidates who win their confidence. But the unhappy events at Chicago's Democratic Convention and the subsequent refusal of many to support Hubert Humphrey have helped lead to the election of Richard M. Nixon. Can we hope that Mr. Nixon and Mr. Agnew will succeed in winning the trust of this generation? The poor? The black? This is surely one of the major challenges of the new administration.

What of the related issue—the insistence of many students that they have an increasing share in governing their own education? For the most part, I confess, I sympathize with them, though once again we must be able to demonstrate, truthfully, that not all things are possible. Many of our brighter students are no longer willing to take part in what they call (sometimes unjustly) "sandbox student government"—by which they mean student organizations with a semblance of power but no real say in the key matters. When students complain that they are constantly told to "think for themselves" and "take responsibility for their courses," are they totally unreasonable in suggesting that such thinking and responsibility may include sharing in decisions about curriculum, faculty tenure, even long-range goals of the institution? Such students, of course, do not at all desire (much less intend) to replace the administrators. They merely point out uncomfortable parallels between colleges which urge students to show initiative but deny them effective power and the white establishment which urges ghetto Negroes to make something of themselves, but maintains control over virtually all of the community organizations. Hence the recent pamphlet with the shocking title *The Student as Nigger*.

The more reasonable among the student rebels do not want administrators to give up their functions; nor do they really resent rules and requirements, so long as these can be shown to be consonant with the professed academic goals of the institution. Many of them can understand the frustration of Columbia's vice-president when he suggested that, if the Vietnam war didn't end soon, the continued existence of his university might be impossible. They understand that colleges have their own distinctive work and cannot become automatic zealots for every strongly espoused cause. They recognize that our colleges have been afforded special privileges and protections precisely *because* it has been recognized that the special obligation of the colleges to preserve the best of tradition and to seek new truth wherever it may lead requires an atmosphere of freedom of thought. And they will see the unreasonableness of those few on today's campuses who will use this special protection to avoid facing the consequences of their own political activities, activities for which all other citizens face inconvenience and some risk. They are, I am convinced, amenable to rational persuasion.

But let none of these considerations be understood to lessen the necessity for today's colleges to assess carefully the legitimate portions of student demands. We would all do well to ponder John Kennedy's observation that those who make peaceful revolution impossible make violent revolution inevitable. I, for one, agree with students that some things can be done to make things on our campuses less impersonal and bureaucratic, if only more imaginative planning of student dormitories. And, if colleges are rightly not political entities per se, they can hardly maintain their professed concern about the ideals of Western culture without paying some attention to institutional stance with regard to social justice. And, considering the increased demands on today's students, college officials may well ask themselves in what legitimate ways they can increase the rewards of academic and personal life while still remaining faithful to their central task.

I do not believe that American colleges are teetering on the brink of anarchy. But there may be tougher times ahead. All who work on campus will need a functioning sense of humor and a commitment to think imaginatively about campus problems. As I have tried to suggest throughout this chapter, it may even be that students, faculty, and administrators can learn to work together to make our campuses better places in which to live and learn. Make plans, not war!

part two

THE PEPSI GENER- ATION?

[Ego integrity] thus means a new,
a different love of one's parents.
  —Erik Erikson[1]
There is no disappointment
we endure one half so great as
that we are to ourselves.
  —Philip Bailey
The Truth must dazzle gradually
or every man be blind.
  —Emily Dickinson
For God knows that when you eat
of it your eyes will be opened,
and you will be like God,
knowing good and evil.
  —Genesis 3:5
Growth is the only evidence
of life.
  —John Henry Newman
He detested the apparatus of piety.
Fusty churches, creaking hymns,
ugly Sunday school teachers and
their stupid leaflets—he hated
everything about them but the
promise they held out ...
  —John Updike[2]
It always rains on our generation.
  —Lucy to Linus[3]

4
GETTING ORIENTED

One of my favorites from "Peanuts" has Charlie Brown complaining: "Life is just too much for me . . . I've been confused right from the day I was born . . . I think the whole trouble is that we're thrown into life too fast . . . we're not really prepared . . ." Linus' reply: "What did you want . . . a chance to warm up first?"[4]

In a way, the college years provide exactly that. New identities, new beliefs, new life-styles can be tried on for size. At the same time, old loyalties are shaken and old ideas roughly challenged. And during these years occurs the almost inevitable crisis of disillusionment. In fact, one of the tests of maturity is the extent to which a person has lost his illusions successfully.

Some people, of course, never get past the stage of disillusionment. Experience can be a bitter pill to swallow. If, when life brings us to a more realistic picture of ourselves, our parents, our society, our inherited religious faith—if then we react with bitterness and cynicism, growth may be stunted. Jesus' verdict in Luke 14:30 about the man who failed to finish building a tower is symbolic of many a life: "This man began to build, and was not able to finish."

Even a passing acquaintance with American literature shows

the importance attached to this theme by our great writers. Hawthorne's young Goodman Brown discovers that his Puritan elders are secretly sinful and the experience warps his life: "A stern, a sad, a darkly meditative, a distrustful, if not a desperate man did he become from the night of that fearful dream." Huck Finn painfully encounters the respectable religion and vicious institutions of Southern society. Hemingway's Nick Adams is forced to come to grips with war and adult complexity. Salinger's Holden Caulfield sees everything as phony, becomes sick of heart and mind. Again and again the theme repeats, in literature and in life: the test of a man's growth is how successfully he has become disillusioned.

Think, to begin with, of the self-disillusionment which faces college freshmen every fall. Being on one's own, of course, has real advantages. But being in the "big leagues" can also be pretty hard on the ego. One freshman wrote this about his orientation period:

> The first time I entered the dining hall of Gore, which was then a freshman dormitory, I went to the nearest empty chair. As I sat down, I said hello to my two or three nearest neighbors. They must at least have looked in my direction. . . . But my clear recollection is that with very little recognition of my presence they went right on talking animatedly among themselves.
>
> What talk it seemed to be! Shaw, Ibsen, Nietzche. . . . Before dessert they had gone on to Katherine Mansfield, and then . . . they dealt, to their satisfaction and mine, with Cabell and Mencken.[5]

Self-doubt is common. That freshman, Nathan Pusey, later became president of Harvard, so all freshmen may take heart. But, for the time being, things may be rough. Was Jim a class president in high school? A commencement speaker? Most likely to succeed? What happens when the midsemester grades roll in, and our hero finds some "C's"? Can he accept a new and more realistic picture of himself? Can he keep on working, even if temporarily discouraged? Will he pass the test that separates the men from the boys, pick himself up, and keep moving? Will he, in short, be successfully disillusioned?

Expand the circle somewhat and consider the almost universal disillusionment of the young with their parents. Could it really be otherwise? After all, to a little child, parents are like gods. When they turn out, over the long haul, to be human beings, there goes another illusion! Young David, in John Updike's moving "Pigeon Feathers," learned all too quickly: "He had never regarded his parents as consolers of his troubles. From the beginning they had seemed to have more troubles than he."[6]

So when parents prove fallible, troubled—even if a person has come from what is called a broken home—the key question is the same: How will the disappointment be handled? Can he learn to accept his parents' failures as well as their successes, their weaknesses, and their strengths; can he learn to relate to them on a more adult level? Or will he strike out in anger and petulance, for years, blaming them fruitlessly for what he feels he's missed. To remain disappointed is to remain in captivity; to grow up is to become successfully disillusioned.

To some extent, this is true with regard to our attitude toward society. If middle age is susceptible to the cop-out, the time-honored role of the young has been to flail out against the false values and hypocritical standards of their elders. It does not take much perception to realize that all that glitters in our Great Society is not gold. Nathan Pusey's comments hit home:

> Not all observers of America in underdeveloped countries accept at face value what we present as a true picture of ourselves—a nation of energetic, independent, happy, free men, intelligently and modestly enjoying one of the highest standards of living ever achieved on this globe. Looking behind our huckster advertising, our self-serving political speeches, . . . they discern, not a nation of happy people living responsibly in a society permeated with justice and mercy, but a national life marred by much frustration and emptiness, hardness and indifference, loneliness and insecurity, selfishness; . . . race prejudice, snobbery of class, irresponsibility, and a host of other evidences of emotional ill health which we minimize, overlook, or pretend to ignore.[7]

Young people do not hesitate to point out that "the king wears no clothes!" The widely distributed Time-Life Report by Sara Greensfelder, *The Young Americans,* contained a solid seam of disillusionment with America. Whether or not one fully agrees with indictments such as the following, we ought to listen and listen carefully:

> I'm sort of sick of the United States . . . the moral standards of most people. Adults in this country are always playing games. They can't do or say what they want. In public, they're forced to be hypocrites by our system, which is all based on money.

> As I began learning more about the state of the country, I began to become very dissatisfied. Aside from corruption, you find that our government is diverting most of its money into useless projects involving the military. . . . Like the whole thing sort of grows, people accept the government and are unaware of what the government is doing.[8]

In the face of an imperfect society, how will today's young react? It is, indeed, a troubled world. When they discover that all nations, including our own, are involved in the world's evil, what will be their response? Callous cynicism? Refusal to get involved? Chronic but aimless protests? I would be among the first to defend the techniques of nonviolent action and protest that have been used in recent years to move us from a societal dead center, but there is no substitute for disciplined effort over the long haul. Dr. William Muehl advises us here:

> The tragic thing about so much of what passes for revolutionary fervor among college students today is that it creates in the student a psychological barrier against a continuing political and social witness in the years ahead. The young man or woman who has learned in college to think of social action as a picnic trip to Washington where, amid the atmosphere of a football pep rally, songs are sung, slogans shouted, and the parietal rules suspended for forty-eight glorious hours of fun and games, such a

student will have little patience with the slow, often boring processes by which a complex nation debates its differences and makes its decisions. It is difficult for a young man who has played the tomcat in his student years to settle down to one woman and a happy marriage. It is no less difficult for one who has had the thrill of marching shoulder to shoulder with throngs of protesting zealots to take his seat in the counsels of elders in the drab halls of our local governments.[9]

Will the protest be one that matters? There are those, remember, who have been successfully disillusioned, and on them rest many of our hopes. College students who have looked squarely at the problems and decided to do something about them are witnesses to the continuing truth of the proverb: "It is better to light one candle than to sit and curse the darkness."

If today's campuses contain more than their share of the all-too-comfortable and selfish, they also contain many who have moved beyond the griping stage. We can only admire those black students who, despite the pull toward separatism or violence, and despite their own bitterness, have continued to join in the struggle to move this country closer toward its dream. We are encouraged by that legion of contemporary missionaries, the Peace Corps, by students who have worked faithfully in off-campus tutorial and poverty programs: all these have met the test of maturity.

Let's admit it, the college experience itself is subject to the same kind of disillusionment. However prettily the catalog describes college life, however strongly lingers the image of the college years as a time of unrelieved joy and excitement, there is a recognizable ring of truth in this comment by a girl from Brooklyn College: "If people are right in saying that these are the best years of my life, then I don't know that I care to stay around and see the rest."

Colleges talk a lot about "preparation for life." But those going to college often wonder just what the curriculum has to do with life, at least life as they experience it. Even assuming that some things which now seem unimportant may seem more useful in perspective (like the first steps in learning a language), also assuming that the curriculum has been fashioned by those with more experience, students will nonetheless find themselves wondering on occasion just what in the world this or that material has to do with their questions and concerns. They may wonder about philosophy courses which seem to shy away from the big questions, about psychology courses which seldom get around to people, about English courses which disavow the significance to literature of the "meaning" of a poem. And they may be less than amused to discover that the word curriculum means "race track," with the strong suggestion of going about in circles.

Moreover, since competition in our colleges often reflects that in our culture, today's student will find himself wondering whether anybody really cares about him as a person. Some gray morning, when he hasn't seen his girl for a month, his roommate's depressed, and an exam is around the corner, he may bitterly question whether he's anything more than a statistic. Does anybody really care?

Inevitably, students discover that professors are people. One may be unduly biased in his approach. Another may be arbitrary and unfair. A third may seem uninterested in teaching. It may come as a shock to discover that these paragons of intellect have feet of clay.

So, when the student's rosy image of academe fades before reality's cold light, then what? Will he transfer? Sleep longer in the morning? Misuse alcohol or drugs to avoid the situation? Or will he learn where the good teaching is taking place, get where the intellectual action is, create with his own enthusiasm and interest the kind of climate he wants? Make no mistake about it, a great deal of what a student gets from the college years depends squarely on him. If he becomes numbed and waits passively for wisdom to seep in by mental osmosis, he may as well go home. To accept the problems and shortcomings of college as well as its strengths, and to make the best of things: that's the key to the growing person.

Students who allow their relationship with teachers to be merely manipulative and superficial would profit from Alfred North Whitehead's book *Aims of Education*, written years ago. Whitehead pointed out that printing and the public library

WILLIAM FINCH

make the modern university unnecessary, *except* as it provides a place to bring together the young and the old in the imaginative consideration of learning. The young bring to the process new premises, energy, stubbornness, and a refusal to give up. The old should bring not only information, but also their own prepossessions, experience, judgment. The magic of education lies in this personal contact between people, and both generations suffer if unnecessary isolation occurs. Working toward this process is worth the shedding of a few illusions.

Growth is vital, too, with regard to one's understanding of religion. Here, too, it is so easy to rattle off the litany of complaints: how bad Sunday school was, a stupid sermon you heard, those hypocrites in the front row at First Presbygational, and all the rest. Let's simply assume that churches, containing people, are fallible. Let's admit that a good deal of conventional "religion" nowadays doesn't command much respect or intellectual assent. Are we willing to move on from there? Having discovered much that appears to us inauthentic, are we willing to work toward a faith that makes sense?

There is a passage in *The Catcher in the Rye* which illustrates the predicament of those who never move beyond rebellion. Holden is fuming about ministers: "If you want to know the truth, I can't even stand ministers. The ones they've had at every school I've gone to, they all have those Holy Joe voices. . . . God, I hate that! They sound so phony!"

But the passage continues: "Anyway, when I was in bed, I couldn't pray worth a damn." There is pathos here, the drying up of spiritual resources caused by immature disillusionment. The question, spiritually, is whether we are able to get beyond the stage of rejecting the false to a believable and workable faith.

Campus conformists never reach this goal. One type of conformist, increasingly rare, comes from a strong church background, seals off part of his mind when he comes to college, keeps his childhood beliefs relatively intact, and takes up where he left off upon graduation. Another type, increasingly common, simply adapts himself to campus conventions. As is frequently the case with his parents, this type does not regard religion as important enough to merit a full-fledged rebellion.

He simply ignores it. He may, of course, ritually condemn it as superstitution, without having studied the matter at a more advanced level than fifth-grade church school. He may imagine himself a freethinker, bravely throwing off the remnants of medievalism; but he is only naïve, and often less than critical in his evaluation of fads and fashions. It is the expected, the conformist thing, to ignore religion on today's campuses. So, if our hero's got everything figured out, he may join happily in the worship of the contemporary trinity: the relativity of all things, the self-sufficiency of man, and the sovereignty of the scientific method in all areas of life.

On the other hand, if he has started to move beyond disillusionment, he may be laying the groundwork for mature faith. It's a slippery and difficult search. What shall I believe? What of conflicting claims? How make sense of the Bible in the twentieth century? What of those who say that God is dead?

It's not likely that here, or in any other areas we've discussed, we'll ever find a complete and finished answer. Life is after all a continuing process, and our growth continues beyond the college years. What's important is the attitude. Keep open, keep looking, reject, select, grow. So we've had illusions? Replace them with something more substantial. Thoreau said it best: "If you have built castles in the air, your work need not be lost; that is where they should be. Now put the foundations under them."

"What is that name?
That name again? Your name?
Who cares?"
　　　　—Edward Albee
So lonely 'twas, that God himself
Scarce seeméd there to be.
　　　　—S. T. Coleridge
All religion, all life, all art,
all expression come down to this;
to the effort of the human soul
to break through its barrier
of loneliness, of intolerable
loneliness, and make some contact
with another seeking soul, or with
what all souls seek, which is
(by any name) *God*.
　　　　—Don Marquis
That is not what I meant at all.
That is not it, at all.
　　　　—T. S. Eliot[1]
We think of the key, each
　　in his prison
Thinking of the key, each
　　confirms of prison.
　　　　—T. S. Eliot[2]

5
ALL
THE
LONELY
PEOPLE

Campuses are deceptive to those who see them only from the outside or on occasional weekends. Those who live there are aware of the desperation behind some of the gaiety. Even the most undisciplined or obnoxious behavior may spring from a core of unhappiness. "If you wanna know where it's at," said my long-haired guide, "listen to the music."

I did, and wasn't too surprised to find the focus on personal relationships, since that's where many are hurting. The prophets of the young sing of tension and anxiety, the gap between the generations, the search for authenticity, the need for love—and, again and again—of loneliness. The Beatles sing of "all the lonely people," of Eleanor Rigby, to whose funeral nobody came, of Father McKenzie, whose sermon no one will hear. All the lonely people.

The Zen scholar Allen Watts, in his book *Psychotherapy East and West,* writes that "man is born with an ego which is in perpetual flight from loneliness and from death." We have it on good authority that "happiness is a warm puppy." Loneliness is all sorts of things—as old as Adam in the garden, as familiar as Jesus being forsaken by his disciples, as contemporary as the man next door. Sometimes it seems that loneliness is a campus—people rushing around like ships passing in the night, interchangeable faces, pasted-on smiles.

Loneliness is a freshman, glad enough to be away from home, but still feeling kind of empty as he walks downtown. There's nothing, after all, when you're by yourself, quite like the "sounds of silence." And in his song Paul Simon gives shape to those sounds, sounds which are the words the lonely people cannot speak or understand among themselves.

But loneliness is not confined to students; it may even be a professor, trying to explain his specialty to his colleagues, and realizing that they're really only half listening. Loneliness can be an administrator, suffering from the stereotypes of his role, and caught between the twin pressures of campus and community.

Loneliness is when people say, "How are you doing?" and then move on quickly—knowing that "a bore is a guy who, when you ask him how he's doing, he tells you." Loneliness is trying to get your parents to understand you and, for that matter, trying to decode them. Loneliness is accomplishing something and being very proud of it and then having nobody pay any attention whatever. Loneliness is showing your girl's picture and meeting dead silence. Loneliness is the "put on," the nervous joke, the whatever-it-is inside of us that makes us need to brag. Loneliness may be an upperclassman, alone in his room, when the concentration comes hard and the routine is suddenly counterpointed by the sound of rain on the window.

> So you sit in lonely silence in your chair
> And watch the roots of sadness growing there.
> Have you ever felt the feeling of the rain
> Like her face shining on your windowpane?
> But there's no one there to share your solitude.
> So you watch the fire shadows in your mood.
>
> And she's gone with the feelings brightly hued.
> And the rain is nothing to help your solitude.
> You see the picture memories from your past
> And take another sip from your glass.
> And it wrecks the thought that you were once so sure
> That time had stopped when she was with you.

But time, my friend, is like a rolling stream
Of rain running down through your dream.
Have you ever felt the feeling of the rain
Like her face shining on your windowpane?
But there's no one there to share your solitude.
So you watch the fire shadows in your mood.

So you sit in lonely silence in your chair
And watch the roots of sadness growing there.

—Rod Von Ohlsen
Franklin and Marshall College
"Have You Ever Felt the Feeling of the Rain?"

Loneliness is being a middle-aged homosexual whom nobody wants. Loneliness is being fat and forty and trying to act like a hippie. Loneliness is being without people and being with people. Loneliness is a student falling behind in his work and afraid to talk with anybody about it. Loneliness is when you're the last one in the room taking an exam. Loneliness is a guy whose girl has just written him a note saying that her school counselor advises breaking off the relationship. Loneliness is going home on vacation and realizing that there are ways in which you can't go home again. Loneliness is when you're a girl on campus and you really like the guy and you wish you could get to know him and all he wants to do is make out. Loneliness is a guy who really likes a girl and is afraid to make a commitment. Loneliness may even be a big campus weekend when the entertainment cancels, the basketball team loses a heartbreaker, and you've got a blind date. Or, loneliness can be going to the game, to the parties, and trying to carry on conversations with your gal and other people—conversations which, somehow, never quite come off. These are the "dangling conversations" of Paul Simon's song, the superficial and unsatisfying small talk of modern life.

Loneliness is J. D. Salinger's Franny Glass, shown to us in *Franny and Zooey*. Near a nervous breakdown, she seeks for help in oriental methods of prayer, then tries desperately to communicate with her insensitive boy friend, Lane Coutrell. Her attempts to establish empathy meet with nothing more

profound than: "If you don't want your butter, I'll eat it."
Franny gives up, faints, locked in by the dullness of another
person.

But loneliness can also be when you really care for someone
and everything is fine . . . and the only thing that hurts is the
separation. Loneliness is missing each other for so long and then
watching the weekend fly by, conscious all the time of the
inevitable parting. Loneliness is when you somehow hurt the
one you love. Loneliness is when you do and say stupid things,
and the words come out all jumbled, and somehow, without
even meaning to, you've hurt her.

> It's a lesson too late for the learnin'
> Made of sand, made of sand.
> In a wink of an eye my soul is turnin'
> In your hand, in your hand.

> Chorus:

> Are you goin' away with no word of farewell?
> Will there be not a trace left behind?
> I could've loved you better,
> Didn't mean to be unkind.
> You know that was the last thing on my mind.

> —Tom Paxton,
> "The Last Thing on My Mind"[3]

Loneliness comes from the walls that we build around ourselves from fear of being hurt, from wanting to love but being
afraid to reach out. The result is people who appear to be
close, but who are in reality worlds apart.

> No . . . it isn't that I want to be alone,
> but that everybody's alone—or so it seems to me.
> They make noises, and think they are talking
>   to each other;
> They make faces, and think they understand each other.
> And I'm sure that they don't.[4]

This age-old problem is intensified in a society which becomes daily more complex, in which people often seem helpless victims of vast and fateful forces. Of course, man has always been afraid of the unknown. Some time ago, a friend directed me to this old Scottish litany: "From ghosties and ghoulies and long-legged beasties and things that go "bump" in the night, Good Lord, deliver us."

That sounds quaint to us, until we read again what the apostle Paul had to say about "principalities and powers," and substitute for "ghosties and ghoulies" the four horsemen of the apocalypse—disease, war, famine, and death—and take an honest look at our world to see how these ancient enemies still ride roughshod over the human spirit. And what about all those strange new forces like automation and cybernation which leave us alternately hopeful and paralyzed?

Loneliness is being an urban Negro male whose family lives (where else?) in the ghetto—wondering wouldn't they be better off without you, since the relief check only comes when you're not there. Loneliness is being a well-intentioned white policeman in the same ghetto, catching hate from both sides, no matter what you do. Loneliness is being a conscientious objector and having others call you a draft dodger. Loneliness is deciding to serve, and discovering that your orders are to shoot first and check the ID card later. Loneliness is being a career officer, neither "dove" nor "hawk" but a guy trying to make a living.

Loneliness is growing old in a system that shoves you aside. Loneliness is discovering that your skills are no longer needed and the world is passing you by. Loneliness is being an old man, living on pension in a small room, wondering whether anyone cares. Are people so caught up in color TV's and their search for pleasure and their priceless sophistication that nobody gives a damn? Thoughts like these can begin to make you a bit peculiar, perhaps like the "peculiar man" of Simon and Garfunkle, who lived alone in a rooming house, and died alone when he decided he could live no longer.

"It has been reported to me," Paul wrote to the Corinthians, "that there is quarreling among you" (1 Cor. 1.11). But the

Corinthians at least met together. Today people are more likely to send a letter to the editor. Loneliness is everywhere. It's being in a position of responsibility, remembering that the buck stops there. It is evoked by Harry Truman's word in 1945 about "the awful loneliness of the White House."

In short, isn't loneliness really part and parcel of the human condition? Isn't loneliness really . . . being human? And don't some of our attempts to dispel it come close to denying our humanity?

To try to avoid loneliness, for example, simply by keeping busy, may be a way of denying our deeper need for love. For if we don't know ourselves, "distracted from distraction by distraction," the speed of the journey doesn't matter much. Thoreau's response to the locomotive was that it might be just "meanness going faster." And Pascal, a brilliant and wonderful man, once said that "all of a man's troubles amount to this, that he cannot sit by himself in a room and think." Going where the action is is useless if we don't know who it is that's going.

To try to avoid rejection and loneliness, on the other hand, by building a shell around the self—does this help either? To love is to risk hurt, to be hurt is painful, to avoid pain is natural. But what is the cost? "No man is an island," wrote John Donne in the seventeenth century, but in plain fact many people are islands. Jesus said to Simon Peter, probably punning, "On this rock I shall build my church" (Matt. 16:18). Those who are familiar with Paul Simon's powerful song "I Am a Rock" will recognize that the "rock" portrayed there is very unlike a community of believers; it is more like a man's own private church, the secret and lonely citadel of the self. A mighty fortress is my . . . self?

How can we receive love if we remain locked up within ourselves? How can we experience joy if we assume no risk of sorrow?

Isn't it also evident that many flee from loneliness at the price of their own identity? Writes Eliot:

> We are the hollow men
>
> . . . .
> Headpiece filled with straw.

. . . .
Shape without form, shade without colour,
Paralysed force, gesture without motion.[5]

Ezekiel's "dry bones," Eliot's "hollow men," Fromm's "marketing personality," Riesman's "lonely crowd"—all describe the man so hungry for acceptance and approval that he works with a series of interchangeable and disposable selves. He wants, above all, like Willy Loman, to be "liked." His values are a function of his immediate environment. He's careful not to have too strong opinions about controversial matters. He wants to be the nice guy. But the Beatles call him "Nowhere Man," the guy with no point of view, no convictions, no plans, no motivation. Nowhere, man!

Finally, let me suggest that loneliness has to do with faith or with the lack of faith. Loneliness is feeling, like Paddy Chayefsky's Gideon, that man is only "a suspension of matter, flailing about for footholds in the void." Loneliness is believing that human destiny is limited to the here and now—that we are insignificant creatures on a small planet of a second-rate sun, making much ado about everything but nonetheless "full of sound and fury, signifying nothing." Loneliness is being a modern man full of interior compartments that box off experience. More poetically, man sometimes seems like:

A bubble on the edge of a vortex
In ceaseless, senseless spin
Part of a foam, bubbles that sparkle and spin.

—Rod Von Ohlsen

Loneliness is being empty spiritually. It's looking for hope and finding a hollow spot. Loneliness is the hell of Edward Albee's Virginia Woolf, the kind of hell which seems the special danger of the well-educated. As David H. C. Read put it, it is a "world of cleverness without compassion, wit without humor, of passion without values, of fantasy unredeemed by faith." The sophisticated cruelty of the games people play do not nurture the spirit. Brittle and cynical postures betray many an empty heart.

So—what about the lonely people? In the end, whose words,

whose theories, whose therapies brilliantly conceived, whose doctrines, whose reassurances, can fill the gap? Perhaps all that we can do is point to the testimony of people who have found warmth, have discovered through learning to trust and give of themselves, that love can, if we let it, dispel loneliness.

> I will love you till the day I die,
> I will love you and I'll tell you why,
> Because your heart is pure, and your
> dreams are mine,
> And I will love you.
>
> I will love you with a love that's true,
> And the only thing that I ask of you,
> Is that you will care for me alone,
> And you will love me.
>
> I will love you till the day I die,
> I will love you and I'll tell you why,
> Because you're life to me, you're just
> right for me,
> And I will love you.
> I love you, I do.
>
> —Rod Von Ohlsen, "I Will Love You"

For many in our day, this is the limit of affirmation: to escape loneliness through the redemptive power of love. Others will testify that there is, in addition, a cosmic loneliness which human love doesn't reach, which yearns for a sense of oneness with the universe. Can we still celebrate the psalms, which take us through all the depths of loneliness and despair, but also rise beyond our human quest on wings of song and trust? Augustine once said, "Thou hast made us for thyself, O God, and our hearts are restless until they come to rest in thee." And many a man will witness that he has not felt complete or whole or healed until he has discovered not only his loved one and his vocation, but, in deep inwardness and conviction, his God.

He began to kiss her.
He thought, It never makes sense.
It is a mystery.
                    —Saul Bellow[1]
Ah, what a dusty answer
    gets the soul,
When hot for certainties
    in this our life.
                    —George Meredith
I've been married eighteen years
and still adore my wife. I have
no hunger for other women; I am
resigned to decency. I actually
think I have found love and life.
What's the matter with me?
                    —John Haynes Holmes
This love of which I speak...
is not possessive: it is neither
anxious to impress nor does it
cherish inflated ideas of its own
importance....It can outlast
anything. It is, in fact, the one
thing that still stands when
all else has fallen.
                    —1 Corinthians 13:4–8,
                        Phillips trans.

6
THIS
THING
CALLED
LOVE

Nothing better illustrates the rapidly shifting nature of our mid-twentieth century than the enormous confusion about sexual ethics and behavior. Who, over or under thirty, can't sympathize with the youngster whose report card showed "F" in deportment: "After all, Mom, conduct is my most difficult subject." Behind the facade of sophistication and big words, that admission remains true for many of us. Conduct, indeed, is our most difficult subject.

The fact is that many ministers, teachers, counselors, and others charged with guiding young adults are frequently not very helpful, if only because they are not in touch with the facts. Harvard psychiatrist Carl Binger writes that sexual morality is: "a tender subject, seldom discussed between the generations. The contemporary sexual mores of young people are so different from those of their parents and teachers that a common meeting ground scarcely exists."

Whether their elders approve or not, many of today's young people are seeking their own rules and rationale for sex. Things are changing and changing rapidly. We ought to face this, not dodge it by reverting to the tired cliché to the effect that every generation has rebelled against the *mores* of its elders. To some extent, of course, that's true. But this observation ought not to blind us to the emergence in the past few years of what Robert Fitch has called the "sexplosion." One need only check his local drive-in movie or corner newsstand or even the late-late show to see the extent to which our culture has become sex-saturated. Sex sells. It is good business. It therefore has our seal of approval. As sober an observer as social scientist David Riesman says: "I insist that there has been a change, a real change, even though you can't prove it statistically. There is an illusion abroad in the land that sex is the most important thing in life and that life can be built on sex alone."

In and out of the churches, the winds of change are blowing. The *"Playboy* philosophy" recounts endlessly the prudery and hypocrisy of conventional attitudes. Some theologians (and several bishops!) suggest that the churches have been peddling an inhuman and outworn morality. Arguing rightly that Christian ethics is never simply a matter of codes, they call for new appraisals and fresh understandings of sex and love in the contemporary world.

Two things at least are crucial: a clear understanding of the current context and, for Christians, an accurate appraisal of the tradition, a sharp look at what H. Richard Niebuhr once called "the minutes of the previous meeting." Sex, after all, is not exactly a new phenomenon in Western history!

Let's begin, then, with a rapid look at the context within which we must make our moral decisions. Let's start by acknowledging that there is something healthful in today's reaction to the extremes of an earlier age. The mother who spoke anxiously to a biology teacher some years ago spoke for too many: "I don't want my Alice to learn nothin' about her insides!" It is hard to estimate the damage to human beings resulting from repressive and guilty attitudes toward such built-in components of the personality as sex and anger. In our culture, indeed, as people feel more and more threatened by loneliness and impersonality, the need for the warmth and security of love (which includes satisfying sex) is likely even more urgent. It is a good thing that theologians are discovering, if somewhat belatedly, the legitimate celebration of the flesh.

Still, thoughtful observers are asking whether today's situation is really therapeutic and human. Will Durant, that wise old historian-philosopher, confesses:

> Most of our literature and social philosophy after 1850 was the voice of freedom against authority, of the child against the parent, of pupil against the teacher. Through many years I shared in that individualistic revolt. I do not now regret it; it is the function of youth to defend liberty and innovation, of the old to defend order and tradition. . . . But now that I too am old, I wonder whether the battle I fought was not too completely won.[2]

One more flaming prophet gone to seed? Are words like these, as Herman Wouk once put it, the "platitudes of maturity?" It is interesting, in any event, to observe the growing number of psychiatrists and others who work closely with people who share Mr. Durant's concern. What do they find disturbing?

For one thing, it seems that we are developing an almost chronic hostility to rules. Hypocritical and senseless regulations have always been fair game for youthful rebels, but more is involved here than that. Some on our campuses openly defend cheating and lying as personal necessities. After all, they say, what's the difference between my final exam and my father's income tax return—or my uncle's expense account? Yet these students are themselves curiously hypocritical—for while they self-righteously flail out at the sins of their elders, they seem to assume that their own cheating, cynical manipulations of others for their own pleasure, and blatant disregard for the feelings of others, are somehow all right. Arguments in support of this kind of behavior gain no more validity from the youthfulness of the source than do their elders' rationalizations deserve the name of maturity.

The same may be said of those who, in regarding themselves as intellectuals, believe themselves to be "above the law"—in particular, above certain social regulations which in their view pertain only to the mass of men. This is an elitist position and it is, in my judgment, an indefensible one. Society itself depends upon a mutually acceptable set of conventions and rules which operate for the protection of all. If rules become outmoded, they may be replaced, but few would argue seriously that men can yet live together successfully without them.

Another disturbing development is a real loss of freedom among many young people, even while talk of the "new freedom" has become common. To be a human being is to be able to make decisions, yet one of the deepest ironies in the current situation is the growing number of forced marriages, unwanted babies, and vocational dead-end streets. The "new morality" obviously yields some familiar old results. It is difficult not to feel genuine compassion and concern for many young people who marry for the wrong reasons, are forced to postpone or curtail their education, or who face the grim choice between abortion or the birth of an unwanted baby. Erich Fromm is quite right in warning that we should not "escape from freedom"; but it is increasingly apparent that there are all sorts of bondages. The fact is: people are getting hurt, often unnecessarily. And students who respond to personalist themes in ethics themselves recognize that our world needs less than anything else another unwanted child.

Again, many are concerned about the growth of that phenomenon sometimes called "privatism." Put simply, the privatist ethic posits the individual as the ultimate and only real measure of the moral life. Morality is entirely a personal affair, and everyone should be free to determine his own code with no reference to social or cultural obligation. As the man says, "It's nobody's damn business but mine!" What a difference there is between a student seriously grappling with the ethical dilemmas of human sexuality and one who cynically maintains that what he does is his own affair—quite similar, I think, to the noticeable difference between the genuine conscientious objector, for whom war is a moral problem, and the privatist student who simply wishes to keep his life from being disturbed.

I have focused here on some of the major problems of the current scene, if only because the "other side" is sure to get a fair hearing. But let me add some affirmative comments. The new honesty is refreshing. It is cold water in the face to societal hypocrisy. How much longer will we overstimulate (in order to sell), then slap? Refreshing, too, is the awareness that the quality of the sexual relationship is basic. No one can overlook those many wonderful kids who build good marriages and make one feel some hope for tomorrow's families. I do not intend to ignore them.

So much for the landscape—a profile of the current scene. Now—how make decisions? What is there in the tradition which still makes sense? What perspectives can students find in the Judeo-Christian tradition that still offer practical and realistic help? Let me venture a few.

To begin with, we misunderstand the biblical perspective on sex unless we begin with the bedrock assertion in the first chapter of Genesis: "And God saw everything that he had made, and behold, it was very good" (Gen. 1:31a). This is the theological North Star, from which any talk about sex in biblical terms must begin. The notion that sex is ignoble or that the body is somehow an "inferior" part of man does justice neither to the best insights of the Bible nor to our contemporary understanding of the complex interrelatedness of body and soul: psychosomatics. God not only made the human body, his act of reconciling and redeeming love was an act of "incarnation," literally "enfleshment."

But let's not rewrite history! There's often a slip 'twixt the text and the application. And while the dualistic view above mentioned is not centrally biblical, we must acknowledge that the total impact of Christian teaching about sex in the Western world has, to say the least, left much to be desired. However theologians have refined the issue from generation to generation, most people gained the general impression from the churches that sexuality was a lesser part of man's makeup. And though some strands of the tradition are better than others in this respect, the church as a whole has richly deserved the rebuke of the contemporary sciences of personality.

Now, however, one wishes that contemporary sexologists would take the trouble to investigate developments within the churches during the last fifty years. Some repeat, endlessly, as the Kronhausens do, that "The Christian point of view regarding sex is based on the principle that sex is permissible only as a means of procreation. It operates with the notion that we are born and conceived in sin. Sex is solely a means to an end and that end is the propagation of the race."[3]

Which Christian point of view? Granted that such views still exist, I have yet to hear an assertion like that in any church I've attended in the last twenty years. One wishes for these authors and for *Playboy's* Hugh Hefner more significant contact with the literature and programs of many of our churches in recent years.

So, to repeat, sex is good, and the pleasure in sex is also good, good in itself and good as it enriches relationships. To teach otherwise is not only bad psychology; it's also bad theology.

Next, let me suggest that sex is for people. That sounds obvious, but isn't. Sex, in human beings, *is* biologically rooted (man is indeed of the earth), but it involves also a whole network of emotional, social, and spiritual factors. The way we use sex reveals our attitude toward others. It measures our maturity. Sex does not "solve" problems of personality; indeed, many unhappy sexual adventures are motivated by the unacknowledged wish for therapy. It is the man unsure of his virility who becomes the Don Juan. It is the girl convinced of her own worthlessness who becomes an "easy lay."

Nor does intercourse magically transform a boy into a man. Students who feel compelled to try sex to prove themselves men may well ask how manly is the need for such reassurance. Girls who feel compelled to yield easily for fear of unpopularity may well question their own opinion of themselves. Nor does control of sexuality cause neurosis. You would be amazed at the number of students I've encountered who have picked up somewhere (any newsstand?) the curious notion that discipline of one's desires would make them mentally unhealthy. That's bad sense—and bad Freud.

Sex is tremendously important to a good marriage, but the relationship is reciprocal, not merely causal. It is not simply that good sex produces a good marriage; rather, it is the maturity and openness of the partners to a good marriage which makes good sex possible. Where human beings are relatively mature and where they are able to relate to others warmly and productively, sex is apt to be a rich and satisfying experience. The quality of the relationship, in other words, determines the quality of the sexual experience.

Let's always remember, too, that sexual intercourse deeply involves another person. "Real life is meeting," wrote Dietrich Bonhoeffer, and this is the point at which the central moral dimension in sex arises. If sex were simply an exchange of bodies, it would have no more moral significance than spitting; nor, one hastens to add, more pleasure! In fact, sex involves another person in one of life's most intimate and profound experiences. The biblical word for intercourse is "know": "Now Adam knew Eve his wife, and she conceived . . ." (Gen. 4:1a). The biblical insight is that intercourse involves a personal knowledge of the other and the corresponding possibility that the other may be radically altered, for better or for worse, by the experience.

Life is "one damned thing after another"; love is "two damned things after another," both human beings. The key ethical question in any transaction is its effect on the people involved. Are "pick-ups" people or just bodies? Is the double standard human: that one type of girl is fair game for intercourse, while another type is a prospect for marriage? By what strange and perverted logic do we continue to place human beings in categories suited to our own desires? Is this really so very different from the judgment that certain people (Jews) are appropriately put in gas ovens? It is clear that much premarital adventuring and extramarital capering involves neither good sex nor true humanity. The human animal is very complex. To be operating at anything near potential, a working partnership among body, mind, and emotion is prerequisite; to divorce these from one another is to court cheapness and neurosis.

"Real life is meeting." Are the *Playboy* girls real or plastic? However much we must commend this manual for its careful attention to young men's preoccupations, we need to recognize the distinction between the real and the false. *Playboy's* bunnies are fantastic, designed to meet the yearnings of those who long for the bliss of sex but are not ready for its responsibilities. It is the immature, the exploiter, who came up with the definition of a perfect girl friend: "A beautiful, blonde, deaf and dumb nymphomaniac who has no relatives and who owns a liquor store." Christian faith, on the other hand, calls us out of fantasyland into the world of living people: "O Living Love, replacing phantasy."[4]

Another thing to remember is that sex and love are not the same thing. The English language is impoverished at this point, having, unlike the Greek, no separate words for erotic attraction, friendship, and divine love. Sex and love (in the sense of deep concern for the welfare of the other person) may go together or they may not. There may be sex with or without love and love with or without sex. "I love you" may often mean "I want you and am therefore quite willing to say I love you," a lesson many a woman has discovered to her sorrow, from the biblical Tamar to the modern coed. "I love her" or "I love him" is, in itself, no justification whatever for a moral position. Dr. Tom Driver's words make sense: "The neon words in this new rhetoric of morality are 'maturity,' 'responsibility,' and 'love.' Actually these statements are so broad (unarguable) that they leave the terrain of moral decision unaffected."

They also ignore our almost infinite capacity for self-deception. Man may be a rational animal, but he is also a rationalizing animal, as any honest person will admit. Erich Fromm, in *The Art of Loving*, wisely removes the word love from the level of sentiment. In human beings, love must be learned. It is "a capacity of the mature, productive character. Is love an art? Then it requires knowledge and effort. Or is love a pleasant sensation, which to experience is a matter of chance, something one 'falls into' if one is lucky?"

Love is not what you start with; it's what you end with. Marriage: for adults only!

Christianity has consistently and rightly held that sex as a casual and fleeting experience is trivial and unworthy of the name love. It has been skeptical of premarital sex and down on extramarital sex not because of an arbitrary code, but precisely because of what happens to the human beings involved. It has held that the best human relationships are based on mutual trust and responsibility, not simply on moods and feelings, and I submit that any new or changed morality will have to come to basic terms with that.

A final observation—"No man is an island. . . ." The words

are seventeenth-century John Donne's, but they are just as true in our world. For better or worse, we are social beings. When it insists that our moral judgments have social meaning, Christian faith is simply being realistic. A national figure embarrasses the administration by becoming involved in a sex scandal. His own business? A marriage is destroyed because of adultery. Their own business? A girl becomes pregnant with no reasonable prospect of marriage. Her own business? His own business?

If so, then why do such situations typically involve ministers, doctors, psychologists, lawyers, adoption agencies, distraught parents, foster parents, and a whole network of complicated community relationships? Our own business? The truth is that our moral decisions determine the kind of people we become. And the kind of people we become will make or break "society." And this is why society has a legitimate concern for the behavior of its members. "No man is an island" . . . ; we effect the human community in one way or another. Not to see this is moral myopia.

It is interesting to examine, as if for the first time, Paul's words in 1 Corinthians 13, the famous "love" chapter. What he is talking about here is mature love, the kind of love deeply concerned about the other, love without an angle, the kind of love, essentially, with which God loves us. The Victorians (so our stereotypes tell us) talked a great deal about love, but knew little of sex. Maybe the time has come for modern Americans, who purport to know a great deal about sex, to rediscover the meaning of love.

Even if you win the rat race,
you're still a rat.
—William Sloane Coffin
The demands of the age are
fashioning the mind of the
university. It ought to be
the other way around.
—Robert M. Hutchins
Therefore I tell you, do not be
anxious about your life, what you
shall eat or what you shall drink,
nor about your body, what you
shall put on. Is not life more
than food, and the body more than
clothing? Look at the birds of the
air: they neither sow nor reap
nor gather into barns, and yet your
heavenly Father feeds them. Are
you not of more value than they?
—Matthew 6:25–26
None of us is Passéd,
we are all Failéd!
—John Barth[1]

7

JUSTIFI-CATION BY GRADE

People who continue to think of the college years as a time of exuberance and boundless optimism had better check in at their local campus for a refresher course. The causes of increased pressure are multiple, but for students they focus most directly on the matter of grades. Clearly, Jesus' sublime words do not seem to belong in today's world; we are convinced that we had better sow and reap and toil and spin—or else!

Or else what? Perhaps a student I once met "booking it" while walking to the residence halls best summed it up. "It can't be that serious," I kidded. Humorless reply: "Oh, yeah? Either I hit *this* one or I've had it!"

He may well have been right. Today's students will not listen long to anyone who tries to soothe their anxieties by assuring them that grades aren't important. They are. That's the kind of a world we live in. We must learn to compete—or else. With solicitous parents prodding and the specter of the draft ever present, nothing can be more infuriating than phony reassurances from people who aren't currently in the academic pressure cooker.

On the other hand, something is clearly wrong in all this.

When grade school children get ulcers, when doctors worry about the widespread use of tranquilizers for children, when college students approach their courses with life-or-death grimness, surely there is distortion. When to fail a course or even get a "C" instead of a "B," when to discover that one is not cut out to be a doctor or can only get into a second-rate graduate school, when these common and sometimes inevitable disappointments become matters of life or death, then I suggest it's time to ask the question about sanity. Which world view *is* crazy, the one which calls us to reexamine our priorities (garbed as it is in language about birds, lilies, and faith), or the one which measures us, tests us, evaluates us, and makes our human security depend on how effectively we can escalate into the affluent society? If students don't go for the birds and lilies approach, they still know intuitively the meaning of the lapel button: "Do not fold, mutilate, or spindle."

It's no secret that many students view their universities and colleges as microcosms of society. They complain about impersonality. They say that colleges make severe demands, but provide little for social and personal enrichment. Students talk about more contact with faculty, but at the same time tend to regard their professors as hurdles to be cleared or minds to be "outpsyched"—in short, as necessary evils to be negotiated on the way to one's degree.

Is this country turning into one vast campus? And are we now justified by *grade* . . . instead of grace? John Barth's fine novel *Giles Goat-Boy* suggests just that. The world is pictured as a great university . . . split into East and West campus. What theologians would have called justification or salvation Barth calls passédness. To be damned is flunkédness, and Barth's "Lord's Prayer" is this:

> Our Founder, Who art omniscient,
> Commenced be Thy name.
> Thy College come; Thy Assignments done
> On Campus as beyond the Gate.
> Give us this term Thy termly word.
> And excuse us our cribbing,
> As we excuse classmates who crib from us.

Lead us not into procrastination,
But deliver us from error:
For Thine is the rank, tenure, and seniority,
forever.
So pass us.[2]

It was interesting to note that when former President Johnson rejected a presidential portrait, the artist said (among other things), "I *flunked* that assignment."

Are we justified by grade? Or, to put it another way, in terms of the Gospel of Matthew, is not life more than *this*? Are we working ourselves into a situation, culturally, where what ought to be accepted as normal failures and disappointments come to us as the crack of doom? No less a person than former Secretary of Health, Education, and Welfare John Gardner confessed, in a speech to prospective collegiates:

> I must say that I worry about the intensity of competition in our good colleges and universities today. I do not believe that college should become a battleground and every day an occasion for triumph or bitter defeat. I hope you will keep in mind that you don't have to win them all. You are going to have a good many setbacks, and some of them will seem fatal and final, but they will not be. The tasks and trials of college test only a *few* of the qualities that make for a successful or significant life. Life is a long, bumpy road, and the prizes go to those with tenacity, durability, resilience, and the capacity to pick themselves up after they take a fall. Have some faith in your long-term capacity to use that ability constructively. Don't let that faith be shaken by momentary setbacks.[3]

In our current context, doesn't that make a great deal of sense? After all, Einstein flunked physics, Caruso was told he'd never be much of a singer, and Jesus of Nazareth was not elected Jerusalem's Man of the Year. Does life totally depend on "making it" in one way or another? Is not life more than this?

Samuel Taylor Coleridge once said, in explaining the perennial power of the Bible, that "there is more that finds me than

I have experienced in all other books put together . . . the words of the Bible find me at greater depths of my being . . . " (*Confessions of an Inquiring Spirit*). Let me suggest that there are at least two things in the passage from Matthew earlier cited which locate us precisely in the midst of our current predicament.

To begin with, notice that the passage strongly certifies our worth as human beings. There is a candid recognition that we need to be approved. Naïve? Perhaps, but magnificently so! Consider how much the obsessive concern about grades and status is rooted just here: the need for approval. Even faculty are strongly tempted to pursue their own advantage instead of pursuing truth. We need approval—and how easily we spot signs that other people don't really care. The suspicion recurs consistently in popular song lyrics, as in Bob Dylan's "Positively Fourth Street," with its bitter attack on social amenities which thinly disguise lack of genuine concern.

Everybody needs approval. In our city a man smashed a bus window with his fist; only later could he get the words out: "Nobody likes me!" Students have a phrase for rejection: "He put me down."

This intense need would seem to be partly natural, partly cultural. When we're children, we learn that some things bring warmth and approval (as important to a child as the sun to a flower); other things do not. How many parents are wise enough and strong enough to provide steady and consistent love? Who but God can love unconditionally?

The need expresses itself in the lingering concern of adolescents that everyone like them. Doesn't it also show up on campuses? Isn't it odd how a student, after submitting a paper or completing an exam, is unable to rest with knowledge acquired or the comforting feeling that he's given it a good try. Instead he haunts the professorial judge: "How did I make out?" (Translate: "What do you think of me?" "Am I really worth something?" "Am I good enough?" "Do you think I'll make it?") Those who suppose that colleges can completely avoid acting *in loco parentis* (in the place of the parent) might question the meaning of this familiar campus drama.

The problem is, of course, that when we are basically unsure of ourselves, that need for approval becomes like a bottomless pit. No matter how much is poured in, it's never filled. And a grade, which ought to be seen as a measure of accomplishment to date, becomes a rejection. It's sort of like being "zapped" by your best friend.

Isn't this part of the reason for the clamor about students being the "forgotten people," about the impersonality of campus life . . . this desperate need for recognition? There is an interesting account by Graham Blaine, of Harvard's Health Services (in *Emotional Problems of Students*), of a student whose work dropped off sharply some months after his father's death. He decided to leave school and travel around the country. The only thing the dean said was, "Fine. Maybe that's best for you right now. I'd like very much to hear from you often, and if you'll supply me with addresses I'll be glad to write." Then something very unexpected happened. Tears. "I didn't know you cared about me."

The academic society is not *meant* to be an arena in which our justifiability as men is to be won by combat. When it becomes that, it can become a living hell, "this damned campus!" No more is a man's vocational success meant to be the primary measure of his justification. The biblical teaching is that a man is to find his basic worth because he is made in the image of God; and the New Testament is clear that we are justified by God's gracious love. But many a man in our culture desperately depends on his work to justify himself as a human being. Why is it that so many fall apart when they retire? Why the psychiatric phenomenon sometimes called "weekend neurosis"? Why such tragic intensity in the plight of those whom automation and technological change make "obsolete"? Does our worth as human beings rest on shifting sands?

Of course discovering a meaningful vocation is important. That's part of what life's about. But doesn't there come a point when a person may justifiably say, not "I am this" or "I am that," but simply "I am"? Is not life more than the grade, the rank, the evaluation? And, as for approval, don't we know that "the Gentiles seek all these things; and your heavenly Father knows that you need them all" (Matt. 6:32)?

Another thing about this passage which may reach us is its introduction. Till now, I've stressed how sublime, how ethereal these words may seem in our kind of world. Reassurance alone may seem unrealistic. But consider this: "No one can serve two masters; for either he will hate the one and love the other, or he will be devoted to the one and despise the other. You cannot serve God and mammon" (Matt. 6:24).

Or, to say it another way: "What will it profit a man if he gains the whole world and forfeits his life?" (Matt. 16:26) For "mammon" substitute the "big slice of pie" waiting for students out there in what some have learned from their fathers to call the rat race. Haven't we learned from Henry David Thoreau that the real cost of a thing is the amount of life that must be exchanged for it? Or from Chaplain William Sloane Coffin that even if you win the rat race, you're still a rat?

Recall that panel in Grossepoint, Michigan, an upper-middle-class neighborhood, in which teachers, ministers, clinicians, all agreed that the high school youngsters there were not only afraid to compete with their successful fathers, but highly anxious that they continue to live in the grand style. In this context education becomes a frightening hurdle.

If many college students have come from relatively plush backgrounds; if, in our society, a college education is almost absolutely essential to escalate the income; if to perform below par in college means sinking in the social scale—then maybe we *are* justified by grade. If we insist on career success and income as keys to a person's worth, then maybe failure to escalate *is* a form of damnation. This damned campus! This damned society!

Perhaps we need to assess our motivation. Could it be that *why* we are in the race is as important as how fast we're running? What does it profit a man if he escalates but loses his personal center of being? What does it profit a professor if he writes five books but loses his own stomach? What does it profit anybody if he gets his slice of pie but loses self-respect? What does it profit any of our institutions of higher education if they gain that elusive thing called excellence and lose concern for human beings?

There is something in our heritage that points to that per-

sonal center of a human being which is more valuable than anything else. Is it possible that more attention to our biblical heritage can provide a "refresher course in the humanities"? The language about human worth and human priorities seems to be awfully important.

Finally, consider the matter of perspective. Just when is life supposed to begin? When exams are over? When we get to graduate school? When we get married? When we have children? When, at last, we have enough income to enjoy life? Or when the children are finally grown up so that we have some time for ourselves? Or is it when we retire? Boris Pasternak puts penetrating words in the mouth of Dr. Zhivago: "Man is born to live, not to prepare for life."

Consider how perspectives change. What seems terribly important and crucial to us now may seem silly ten years from now. Today's unnecessary anxieties may be tomorrow's jokes. In terms of human happiness, I much suspect that some things quite apart from academic and professional life will prove even more important: the kind of marriage one has, the children, the way in which we learn to deal creatively with disappointments and setbacks.

In 1984, George Orwell pointed to a rapidly diminishing commodity called "ownlife." When that disappears, what that is human remains? We must continue to insist that our chief value lies in the simple fact of creation: we are, indeed, human beings.

There is a moving conversation in *Don Quixote* between Sancho Panza and his wife Teresa. Panza, led on by the Don's fancies, confesses to his wife: "If I did not expect to see myself governor of an island before long, I would drop down dead on the spot." (Med school or bust?) Teresa replies:

> Nay then, husband, you came out of your mother's womb without a government, you have lived until now without a government, and when it is God's will, you will go, or be carried to your grave without a government. How many are in the world who live without a government, and continue to live all the same, *and are reckoned in the number of the people.*

And are reckoned in the number of the people! Consider the many ways in which our culture will continue to measure and rank us; are we not of more value than they? And, in the long run, whether in each instance we are passéd or flunkéd may be considerably less important than whether we manage to become reasonably happy and productive human beings.

To current and prospective students: Maybe you aren't the genius of the age; but you have a solid contribution to make, and you're more likely to make it if you retain both your sanity and your digestive tract. Chart your course carefully, drive skillfully, but *you* drive; don't be driven. It's not at all likely that the universe is on *this* kind of a pass-fail system. And we have it on good authority that it profits us little if we gain cherished goals at the cost of our integrity or our very lives.

ANNA KAUFMAN

part three
WHAT'S IT ALL ABOUT?

If it wasn't for Christianity
Negroes would have stopped praying
a long time ago. They would have
started raising a whole lot of hell.

> —Claude Brown, *Manchild
> in the Promised Land*

When there is hunger, God is an
escape from a harsh reality. When
there is freedom from hunger, God
is a harsh but inescapable reality.

> —William Sloane Coffin

Little by little we subtract
Faith and Fallacy from Fact,
The Illusory from the True,
And starve upon the Residue.

> —Samuel Hoffenstein[1]

Well, sir, if you think of all
those illusions that mean nothing
to you now, of all those things
which don't even *seem* to you to
exist any more, while once they
were for you, don't you feel
that...all this present reality
of yours...is fated to seem
a mere illusion to you tomorrow?

> —Luigi Pirandello,[2]
> *Six Characters in Search
> of an Author*

8
IS
RELIGION
A
CRUTCH?

No one has really come to terms both with faith and modern culture unless he has confronted the truth in the Marxist-Freudian assertion that religion is an illusion, a crutch needed by the weak in an imperfect world. On today's campuses, the implications of that assertion present a major challenge to believers.

Let's face it squarely: Is faith an illusion? It would often seem so. Against the background of our time Christian faith seems to many mere wishful thinking, a pleasant escape. The realities of life seem so unbendable and religion so much part of a dream world that John Updike's description of some versions of faith is apt: "a pastel forest designed for a fairyland romp."[3]

How many of us are not sometimes haunted by this suspicion? It is true enough that faith is comforting and sustaining. It is indeed subjectively helpful to those who believe in it; but is it true? Is it real? After all, life is a grim business much of the time, and people are not to be blamed if they seek illusion, as does the poor woman in Robert Lynd's *Middletown:* "Land sakes! I don't see how people live at all who don't cheer themselves up by thinkin' of God and heaven."

That says it well. Religion is a kind of chloroform mask, as one student put it, into which the weak and unhappy stick their faces.

The charge is not new. It has its roots in the ancient world. And in modern times, fifteen years before Sigmund Freud was born, Ludwig Feurbach wrote: "Religion is the dream of walking consciousness; dreaming is the key to the mysteries of religion." Karl Marx added that religion is but the "opiate of the people," promoted by the rich to keep the poor happy; and the Anglican Church of his day proved his point by meriting its well-known description of "the conservative party at prayer."

And then there was Freud. This remarkable man spent most of his life working with pathologically disturbed people, reaching thereby insights of enormous importance. He noticed that, in his patients, religion functioned as a kind of socially approved neurosis. Some of his patients looked on God as a cosmic grandpa who would help them in any emergency. Freud concluded, in *The Future of an Illusion:*

> Religion is an attempt to get control over the sensory world . . . by means of the wish world. But its consolations deserve no trust. Experience teaches us that the world is not a nursery. . . . Psychoanalysis has taught us that the personal God is, psychologically, *nothing other* than a magnified father.

Thus Freud focused for our day the ancient and perennial cry: is not religion *merely* a crutch for the weak, an illusion of the impotent? Should not modern man turn from the wish world and confront reality openly, courageously?

The answer, I submit, is yes. While we need to guard against facile generalizations (as in "merely" and "nothing other"), we ought in all honesty to plead guilty as charged on behalf of a good deal of religion, past and present. For isn't it so that much of what passes for faith in our day looks for all the world like a desperate attempt to avoid the harsh realities of life—pain, sacrifice, transiency, death?

The great awakening of young Negro Americans in the past

few years, their growing indignation with churches which have lulled the poor and miserable with consoling recourse to the "sweet by-and-by," their insistence that the churches deal with the urgencies of *this* life—this contains a lesson for all of us, vividly underlined by the violence following the tragic death of Dr. Martin Luther King.

Try an experiment. Take any Sunday's *New York Times*; clip out all references to religion and the churches. A pattern clearly emerges: there are, it appears, two kinds of religion in today's world. Religion A conducts business as usual. It apparently centers on the tired preoccupations of Protestant pietism: Sunday movies, drinking, the dangers of miniskirts, and the supremacy of those old-fashioned virtues associated with "the Protestant ethic." Beyond acts of individual charity and a lingering concern for the benighted heathen in faraway lands, the churches of Religion A give little sign that they are a part of our world—except for an occasional social action visit to city hall if a tavern opens within a few blocks of the church building.

Thank God there is also Religion B. Obviously I'm exaggerating its virtues, but the difference is so striking. The churches of Religion B take their world seriously. Sometimes enterprising individuals (clergy and laymen) are viewed with suspicion by the majority of the membership, but there is a heartening indication that a growing number of people in American church life are simply unwilling to set up business at the old corner. While the front page of the Sunday *Times* screams of a world in anguish and confusion, Religion A virtually ignores it; Religion B (also with confusion!) tries, at least, to face the issues.

Some time ago I was interviewed by a reporter doing a story on young people and church attendance. She reported to me that local pastors were concerned about high school ecclesiastical dropouts and wondered how things were in the colleges. My opinion was that there are three major stances among today's college students. First of all, there are a large number of students (often following the example of their parents) who have had and will have little or nothing to do with their churches and synagogues. Was it Mark Twain who observed that human nature is very prevalent? Let's face it, a great many people are preoccupied with themselves, their private goals, their personal pleasures. Then there are those who may or may not have done much about organized religion during the college years, but are not really hostile to the churches. Many of them will probably join, following graduation, if only because our society urges us to belong to something and because of "the children."

But the *leaders* of this college generation—the kind of students who have been involved in serious study, in civil rights activities, in the war on poverty and the peace movement—these, in my opinion, hold the key to the future of the churches. And many of them will simply not join a church for the sake of joining. The routine organizational patterns of many of our churches will bore them to tears. Mildly respectable but innocuous projects—bazaars, ham suppers, raising money for a new wing of the educational plant, discussion groups which never go beyond discussion, committees which give the illusion of activity but accomplish little—all these will leave them cold. Sermons which merely pass along what John Kenneth Galbraith has called "the conventional wisdom" will put them to sleep. But where there is vitality, where a minister and a core of the congregation are seriously attempting to confront community and society, where there is honest and open attention to real problems, where there are Christians who care less about building projects (the edifice complex?) than they do about human justice and compassion, there the possibility of enthusiasm on the part of today's college students is very much alive. If the churches are open enough and willing to face the fact that you can't make omelets without breaking a few eggs, they will discover a solid core of the committed, those who, in Studdert-Kennedy's memorable phrase, will "remain explosively within the church."

It is crucial that we face this issue. Any religious tradition can be misused. Certainly parts of the Bible lend themselves to an escapist interpretation. Consider, for example, Psalm 91:3-7:

For he will deliver you from the snare
    of the fowler
  and from the deadly pestilence;
he will cover you with his pinions,
    and under his wings you will find refuge;
    his faithfulness is a shield and buckler.
You will not fear the terror of the night,
    nor the arrow that flies by day,
nor the pestilence that stalks in darkness,
    nor the destruction that wastes at noonday.
A thousand may fall at your side,
    ten thousand at your right hand;
    but it will not come near you.

One wonders how chaplains of combat units in Vietnam would use this passage! And our conventional notions of prayer—do they not often suggest the image of God as a celestial bellhop? Isn't much of what is called prayer simply magic, the attempt to persuade the Almighty to see things our way? Prayer: "Thy will be done, through me"; magic: "My will be done, please, through thee." Prayer is not Aladdin's lamp and we must ever be on guard against what Kierkegaard called "twaddle in the Holy of Holies." The pernicious business of using religion to our own unworthy ends is at least as old as the biblical Jacob: "If God will be with me, and will keep me in the way that I go, and will give me bread to eat and clothing to wear, then the Lord shall be my God" (Gen. 28:20–21). Add, for our own era, the guarantee of "peace of mind," the maintenance of the status quo, or the use of right-wing religion to bolster economic conservatism, and the picture rounds out. I owe to a colleague this tongue-in-cheek ditty which makes the rounds at Dartmouth's Tuck School of Business:

God bless Free Enterprise,
System Divine,
Stand beside Her, and guide Her,
Just as long as the profits are Mine.
                (to the tune of
            "God Bless America")

One of our errors has been to confuse religion-in-general with authentic, biblical faith. If all we want from faith is a divine protector of our privileges, a sure refuge against the consequences of our own stupidity, a convenient *deus ex machina* to bail us out in emergencies—then we are acting not in faith but in selfishness and superstition.

As a matter of fact, the Bible is pretty rough on "religion." With whom did the prophets have the most trouble? Was it not precisely with the little cults, established on every hilltop to promote one or another special interest? With whom did Jesus quarrel? Was it not, most frequently, with those who used the cloak of religion to guarantee their pride and privilege? Indeed, much of the Bible seems to be in the same business as Freud: illusion-shattering! Will Herberg makes some helpful distinctions:

> "Religion qua religion" is concerned with bolstering man's self-esteem and security in the face of a hostile universe; biblical faith is concerned with shattering all human securities and bringing man, in "fear and trembling," face to face with God. Among the human securities that biblical faith is out to shatter is the very security that religion is designed to bring. In this sense, it is quite true that biblical faith is "antireligious"; it is indeed a faith whose very purpose it is to "end" all religion and bring man directly under the command, judgment, and redeeming grace of God.[4]

A practicing Catholic psychoanalyst, Gregory Zilboorg, wrote several years ago that men nourish two major illusions: that they are completely free and that they are immortal. Religion, he suggested, is a human attempt to provide guarantees to support such illusions. Zilboorg was being profoundly biblical; freedom and eternal life are gifts of God to those who stand in a faith-relationship to him. They cannot be "won" or automatically assumed, nor do they function as cosmic life insurance. I suggest that contemporary Christian faith owes a tremendous debt to those who have correctly and forcefully pointed to its neurotic distortions, and not the least of these was Sigmund Freud. There is a story told about Bishop Pike, occurring during his ministry at St. John's Cathedral in New York City. Among the stained-glass windows to be dedicated was one portraying the founder of psychoanalysis. It is reported that a lady, much upset about this, gasped: "He wasn't even a Christian!" Pike's retort: "He is now, madam."

There is, of course, another side of the coin. Freud, like all men, was a prisoner of his age. We live in a time when the confident scientism of some years back has been severely shaken. And we have come to see that all men operate by faith, hidden or acknowledged. It is the quality of the faith that counts.

Further, there is a sense in which we do need supports, call them crutches if you will. An atheist, it has been said, is a man without any invisible means of support. Nor is it neurotic or escapist to draw upon faith's resources when one is also open to the world about him. Most people are, in fact, crippled in one way or another. Freud once said that no man is unburdened with the precipitate of the Oedipus complex. But whether or not you can accept the Freudian mythology, it takes little insight to observe that most people carry within them conflicts and burdens.

Do you recall the account, in the second chapter of Mark's Gospel, of the paralytic brought by his friends for healing? Three things seem significant: that the man was crippled and needed a crutch; that there were apparently psychosomatic complications, since the healing had something to do with the forgiveness of his sins; and the instructive order of Jesus following the healing, "Rise, take up your pallet and walk" (Mark 2:9b). No more free stretcher rides! No more tender loving care! On your feet, report at eight!

If we read the Gospels carefully, as Leslie Weatherhead has reminded us, we find they are full of comfort and consolation, full of assurance that we are loved; but there is no word of comfort that does not involve a challenge. "Come unto me" (Matt. 11:28a, KJV), says the inviting voice, but also: "Go ye out into all the world" (Luke 16:15, KJV). One of Freud's startling discoveries was that the moment of greatest resistance to therapy comes when the patient is at the doorway to health. The new self, the healed self, is frightening; it brings with it new demands, new responsibilities. Religion, wrote Reinhold Niebuhr, is to comfort the afflicted and afflict the comfortable!

There is, to be sure, a passive, receptive side of life, reflected beautifully in Whittier's familiar lines:

> Drop thy still dews of quietness,
> Till all our strivings cease;
> Take from our souls the strain and stress
> And let our ordered lives confess
> The beauty of thy peace.

The Western world, yes, Christianity, is paying dearly for neglecting that side of life. The intense fascination of the young with Zen and other forms of Eastern religion, the cult of "transcendental meditation," the quest of hippies for expanded consciousness and a deeper life of the spirit—these are by no means all faddish and esoteric. They reflect our ignoring of the comtemplative and the extent to which our technological era exteriorizes, depersonalizes, thwarts spontaneity.

The full life needs both dimensions. Whittier, good Quaker that he was, charted the beauties of the inner life. But he also stood at Concord, speaking against slavery, pelted by rotten eggs, lampooned as a traitor to his country.

No man who enters seriously into Christian commitment will find there superficial comfort; he will discover, instead, a deep and disturbing command. Freud talks as though men invented a God to calm their fears. Some men doubtless do, but not all men. That fisherman, Peter, who was crucified upside down, was his faith a pleasant escape from reality? Or Paul, the scholar who chose a life of extreme danger and, for his pains, was beheaded. Or our Lord—he had feelings; his was no suicidal wish. Yet he prayed, "My Father, if it be possible, let this cup pass from me; nevertheless, not as I will, but as thou wilt" (Matt. 26:39b). Is this kind of faith "a pastel forest designed for a fairyland romp"? Jesus was offered a religion of escape in his forty days in the wilderness; he did not pick up the option.

Before we talk too glibly about crutches, we had better look at our own. Some men need perpetual bolstering with large doses of alcohol. The stresses of life have others on pills, legal and illegal. Others seem to need to degrade their fellows to boost their own egos. What's this about crutches?

At its best, faith brings courage. "The authentic Christian experience," writes Leslie Weatherhead, "is a courageous trafficking with reality . . ." And while it is not hard to find examples of escapist evasion in Christian history, it is sheer blindness to fail to recognize that key role in Western culture of men who have combined faith in God with transforming personal courage. In *Young Man Luther*, Erik Erikson writes, "Luther and Freud both showed a grim willingness to do the dirty work of their respective ages." An entry in David Livingstone's diary reads: "Took up three holes in my belt to relieve my hunger." Nor can one ignore those contemporary heroes of the civil rights movement, supremely Martin Luther King, the knight of faith who prayed with his eyes wide open, who never let the mount of inspiration supplant the valley of decision. And who in our time can forget the courage of the Kennedys during two shocking assassinations and fail to see that the substance and power of faith made much of it possible?

The question about religion is always ultimately personal. Is faith an illusion? How about yours?

How dreadful knowledge
of the truth can be when there's
no help in truth.
            —Sophocles
He who increases knowledge
increases sorrow.
            —Ecclesiastes 1:18b
[Man] made two mistakes.
One was to stand up and the other
was to start thinking. It strains
the spine and the nerves.
            —John Updike
The knees were meant to bend,
but not the head.
            —F.-M. Voltaire
Here is no water but only rock
Rock and no water and the
    sandy road.
            —T. S. Eliot[1]
Lift up your head and hark,
    what sounds are in the dark;
For his feet are coming to thee
    on the waters.
            —Francis Thompson

9

WOULD YOU BELIEVE... TRUTH?

My question here is simple: Can a person, in matters of religious faith, find the kind of truth which is believable and dependable?

We tend to be highly suspicious of abstract words like honor and glory and truth. Truth: Well . . . would you believe a high probability? An educated guess? How about a shot in the dark? Maxwell Smart's comical reductionism usually punctures his own inflated balloons. But the doubt behind the humor is a familiar one to many of us.

It is important that we confront this problem because the mood is powerful among us that the only decent, respectable truth is that which can be verified by the evidence of the senses. And if our faith can lay no claim to valid truth in the midst of the current knowledge explosion, it would seem that for serious and thoughtful people it is likely to become the relic of a bygone era.

As a way of exploring this question, consider the words of Jesus, as recorded in John's Gospel: "If you continue in my word, you are truly my disciples, and you will know the truth, and the truth will make you free" (John 8:31b–32). I have found these words useful in considering the implications of the search for truth in matters of religion.

To begin with, don't these words of Jesus suggest that there are different kinds of truths? Clearly, Jesus is not speaking here of the kind of truth which becomes available to the scientist after patient hours in his laboratory. Nor that which occupies a philosopher delving into the uses of language. The truth referred to here has more to do with the center of personal decision and response.

Michael Polanyi, in his book *Personal Knowledge*, helpfully distinguishes between two different kinds of knowledge; he calls them articulate and inarticulate. Articulate knowledge is the kind which is involved in our description and explanation of the natural world. So clear and precise is this knowledge that some claim it to be the only reliable knowledge we have. But Polanyi argues persuasively that there is also "inarticulate" knowledge, the kind we have, for example, of ourselves and of other people. This is even more important to us as persons; but it involves a different way of knowing.

Nothing but confusion and frustration comes from mixing these two kinds of truth. We are comfortably accustomed to scorn the old-style fundamentalism, with its narrow-minded and dogmatic approach. It ruled out whole areas of truth. But there is a *new* on-campus fundamentalism, as Nathan Pusey has so forcefully reminded us, that is just as dogmatic and partial. It is the fundamentalism of those who are so impressed with the results of the scientific method that they relegate all other truths (in religion and in the arts, for example) to inferior status. Pusey's essay in *The Age of the Scholar* is a wise reminder that we need not submit to the tyranny of the tangible.

Let's put it on a more personal level. When we get around to asking the questions which concern us most as human beings, where do they fall? Are they the kind of questions which can be answered by an objective, thoroughly analytical approach?

Erik Erikson is a psychiatrist who has written penetratingly about what is involved in reaching maturity. Without using his precise terminology, I think one can summarize Erikson's position by stating that one achieves a meaningful identity in the process of finding: (a) someone to love, (b) something to do, (c) something to believe.

What kind of truth is involved here? How do we find someone to love? How do we *know*? Well, the entrepreneurs of "Operation Match," with their computerized dating service, are trying to reduce all possibility of risk and human choice. To cite one of their come-ons: "What's your type? Blond, redhead? Vivacious, suave? Debonaire, whimsical? Challenging, dumb? Sexy, petite? Warm, cool? Whatever it is, it can be yours by computer."

Will this solve the search for a life partner? And how will we find something to do—our vocation? How will we know what's right for us? Why is it that it's often so excruciatingly difficult for us to pick and choose something that looks worth doing? How do we feel, in the midst of this kind of dilemma, when someone cheerily asks us to objectify the problem? "Now you go take an aptitude test!"

It is clear, isn't it, that getting at the "truth" in these situations of personal perplexity is quite a different thing from the approach one might use in a laboratory.

The same is true of the third area of decision, that of finding something in which to believe. What is involved is one's decision about the meaning of life, its highest values, its deepest aspirations. And it is at this level, I suggest, that we can understand the kind of truth addressed in Jesus' words: "If you continue in my word, you are truly my disciples, and you will know the truth, and the truth will make you free."

Another thing these words suggest is that there are conditions for getting at the truth here in question: "If you continue in my word . . . you will know the truth."

This shouldn't come as a surprise. Doesn't truth of all kinds have conditions? Aren't there conditions, rigorous and demanding ones, for getting at truth in the laboratory? Aren't there conditions for profound understanding of music, or art, or just about anything?

Luke's story about Jesus and the man with the withered arm provides some good clues to the conditions for spiritual integrity. You will remember that the Pharisees were trying to trap Jesus concerning the matter of healing on the sabbath.

This was a live issue for them; to understand their urgency we might substitute mentally the question of our involvement in Vietnam, or the intricacies of "black power." Jesus brings the crippled man before them, and knowing their preoccupation with the legality of the matter, he says: "I ask you, is it lawful on the sabbath to do good or to do harm, to save life or destroy it?" Note the question at issue: What is the correct way to observe the sabbath? What is the *truth* here?

A few years ago, Conrad Massa pointed out that Jesus' response may well indicate *his* criteria for truth in religion. Look, for example, how he reshapes the question so that it becomes a *moral* one rather than solely *intellectual*. The Pharisees wanted to ask: "Is it permitted to work on the sabbath?" The answer was in the back of the book. They would find out by searching the law. It was an intellectual task.

Jesus changes the question. "Is it permitted to do good or to do evil?" This is a moral question.

Aren't we really like these Pharisees? Wouldn't we much rather keep the religious question at a safe level—an intellectual level? "What do you think about God?" "Come over tonight, we'll have a bull session about religion."

Doesn't Jesus' response in this story suggest that truth in matters of faith may involve as much a moral as an intellectual dimension?

Look at our common life. We ask these questions: Aren't Negroes going too far? What happens to the value of housing in areas where Negroes move in? Why are all those people on the relief rolls? Why is it up to us to give money to other countries?

That's one way of posing the questions. Would Jesus switch categories on us? Would he have us ask, instead, what it feels like to be a victim of continuing white supremacy? Might he ask: Who is your neighbor? Do you know how it feels to be poor or hungry?

The Pharisees wanted it according to the book; Jesus, according to the life.

Ask the questions about sex: Isn't it true that sex mores in other cultures are much different from ours? Don't changing social codes make premarital intercourse acceptable nowadays?

Aren't we like those Pharisees, asking according to the *mores*, checking for possible loopholes in the law? Would Jesus ask, instead: How are you treating this girl? Why are you dating her? And again: Who is your neighbor? On Christ's terms, it appears that the search for truth has a *moral* dimension.

The other thing that Jesus does in this story is reverse the whole *context* of the question. The Pharisees wanted to keep the incident at a level of objective theory. This man, this poor fellow with the withered arm, was a test case. What would Jesus *do* in a case like this? Interesting!

There are some kinds of knowledge, of course, which require detachment and objectivity. But there are whole areas of life where this posture is inappropriate, even destructive. Søren Kierkegaard, in one of his vivid parables, tells of the ever-present temptation to become spectators and detached observers. He imagined that near the cross of Christ stood a man who witnessed the crucifixion and, thereafter, became a professor specializing in what he had beheld. Quite clearly, urbane detachment does not get us to the deepest truth about man and God. Jesus confronts his man as a man, at the level of personal involvement.

He felt for him. He healed him—and not without risk. "They were filled with fury and discussed with one another what they might do to Jesus" (Luke 6:11).

These are two helpful clues, I think, toward getting at these truths which are most important to us as human beings. They are more *moral* than intellectual; and they require *personal involvement*.

Apply this now to our basic human decisions. Will one ever find someone to love without a risk, without a personal decision? "Marriage," as somebody said, "is one of those decisions in life that have to be made on the basis of insufficient evidence." Yet decide we must or remain single. And can we ever be totally sure of our "true" vocation before taking the leap? The evidence may seem painfully insufficient, yet leap we must —or remain paralyzed. A personal decision is required before we can share the kind of knowledge that comes in a loving human relationship—or the kind that comes in the feeling of productive work well done.

If in these matters the evidence is inconclusive, and requires our personal involvement and risk, why should we expect otherwise of faith? "*If* you continue in my word, you are truly my disciples, and you will know the truth, and the truth will make you free."

So the truth which Christ speaks of is deeply personal truth; it demands moral concern and involvement. There is one more thing which can be said about it: It is liberating. "You will know the truth, and the truth will make you free."

This verse has been the occasion for endless baccalaureate sermons and commencement addresses, many of them, I might add, conveniently ignoring the conditional clause which precedes it. It is important to the academic quest, since it suggests forcefully that religious commitment is no enemy to the life of the mind.

As you may know, Simone Weil refused to enter the Roman Catholic Church, despite deep personal longings, for fear of losing her intellectual freedom. And many a believing Christian can sympathize with the agony of Teilhard de Chardin, whose brilliant work could be published only posthumously. But if the past record of the churches has been tarnished, we need remember that the scientists of Darwin's day and the medical men of Freud's were equally opposed to new truth. Faith must acknowledge its William Jennings Bryans and its Carl McIntires, its Billy James Hargises and its flat-earthers. But faith also claims SS. Augustine and Aquinas, Luther and Pascal, de Chardin and Marcel, Dorothy Sayers and C. S. Lewis, the Niebuhrs and Tillich—men and women who have combined high intelligence with responsible commitment. Indeed, some of the most creative intellects of the Western world have been people deeply committed both to religion and to the life of the mind, and many of them were Roman Catholic. It was no accident that many of our colleges were born of the churches.

Faith can indeed be liberating; indeed, one may question whether a religious position which does not have a creatively liberating effect on the mind and spirit even deserves the name of faith! One reason for this is seldom, if ever, mentioned. It is simply that a freely chosen commitment liberates enormous amounts of energy which theretofore had been spent in the struggle.

This is not to suggest that anyone ever "arrives," in the sense of achieving static perfection. In all areas of life, we must continue to grow or we begin to die. But, to return to our central examples, isn't it true that the young man who finally finds the girl of his dreams—and discovers, with her, the joy of building a marriage—isn't it so that he is then free to turn some of his attention to other matters? How many a parent or long-suffering roommate has muttered in relief, "Thank God, he's finally married!"

And isn't it also so that a successful resolution of the vocational problem releases a lot of productive energy which has been tied up in the search? Again, if a man is able to make an authentic religious commitment, is he not a freer man? Part of the freedom that intelligent commitment should bring is the freedom from excessive self-preoccupation, tortured doubts, and the compulsive navel-gazing which seem so characteristic of our time? Doesn't alienation create its own kind of bondage?

In any event, it's interesting to see this theme picked up in modern literature, as character after character views "thinking" as a terrible enemy. "You shall know the truth," says one of Cozzens' characters in *By Love Possessed*, "and the truth will make you sick." Melville's works provide numerous illustrations, notably Starbuck's sentence in *Moby Dick:* "The one commandment is: Thou shalt not think." And consider the Hemingway hero, despairing of life, intent on dispelling the giant Thought with excessive doses of violence and compulsive sexuality. What kind of freedom is this? Is it possible, finally, that the person with *no* base to touch is so insecure that he *cannot* think freely?

These words of Jesus remind us that his truth is deeply personal; that it has its conditions; and that the invitation is not only to the naïve and uninformed, but to complicated modern man, smack in the middle of his dilemma: "If you continue in my word, you are truly my disciples, and you will know the truth, and the truth will make you free."

We are ... perplexed,
but not driven to despair.
　　　　—2 Corinthians 4:8
A solid agnosticism, even more
than a solid faith, requires
a stable world, one indeed that
is on the march to a rational
paradise. People might have
believed this when John Dewey
was a boy.
　　　　—Paul Goodman[1]
No, really, Herr Nietzsche,
I have great admiration for you.
Sympathy. You want to make us able
to live with the void. Not lie
ourselves into good-naturedness,
trust, ordinary middling human
considerations, but to question as
has never been questioned before,
relentlessly, with iron
determination, into evil, through
evil, past evil, accepting
no abject comfort.
　　　　—Saul Bellow[2]

10
THE
CRISIS
OF
BELIEF

There is no campus problem more important than the problem of meaning. Those who judge the intensity of concern for religion by calculating the constancy of church attendance or the degree to which students retain the beliefs of their parents misread the situation. Though their present and future relationship to what they call "organized religion" is problematic for many of the young, there is no struggle which is, for the serious, more difficult or painful than the attempt to find something solid by way of faith. All of the other dimensions of campus life we've discussed are related, in one way or another, to this search. A student riot at Princeton a few years ago brought the following thoughts from a boy soon to be graduated:

The trouble with me is that I can't believe in anything. On some days I can, but most of the time I'm smarter than that. I have been taught to question, not to believe, so I never know where to stop. . . . What I want is a cause; what I cannot have is a cause, because I know that causes are the opiate of the masses. . . .

> This, in essence, has been my Princeton career: running after education, which supposedly begets progress, while at the same time learning that progress is the apple dangled in the face of the draft horse. I am therefore unable to define myself. The best I can do is delimit myself, without guilt or joy.[3]

While that young man does not speak for all, there is no question that the task of forging out believable convictions is a painful and strenuous one for many of today's students. It is understandable that a great many seem to abandon the effort; indeed, the very indifference and blasé attitude of some may indicate that this is a painful area, best denied; and the open and intense hostility to religion (found today more often among faculty than among students) is another tip-off that for many in our culture the search for belief has ended in pain and disappointment. Barth's parody (in *Giles Goat-Boy*) has the sting of truth:

> Many semesters ago, in what history professors call the Rematriculation Period, the old West-Campus faith in such things as an all-powerful Founder and a Final Examination that sent one forever to Commencement Gate or the Dean o' Flunks had declined. . . . There had been, it appeared, no Foundation-Day: the University had always existed . . . ; moral principles were regarded by the Psychology Department as symptoms on the order of dreams, by the Anthropology Department as historical relics on the order of potsherds, by the Philosophy Department variously as cadavers for logical dissection or necessary absurdities. The result (especially for thoughtful students) was confusion, anxiety, frustration, despair, and a fitful search for something to fill the moral vacuum in their quads.[4]

What shall a student believe? Which of the equally intelligent and persuasive voices he hears shall he follow? The tower of babel still rises on the lawns of academe, and the diversity of languages is still as baffling. Further, the major religious traditions in this country are undergoing "identity crises" themselves, and the tumultuous nature of the questions and changes make it even harder for the young to decide which course to follow. The churches seem beset with twin temptations: to return to the old and familiar out of anxiety, thereby cutting themselves off from needed correctives; or to plummet dizzily toward the latest word off the presses, with some confidence that what is new is better. It is not likely that either approach will merit much respect among more experienced members of our college communities, but it is not surprising that the whole scene looks pretty bizarre to undergraduates!

Michael Harrington, author of *The Other America*, recently gave some "radical advice" to "radical religionists." He suggests that no genuine reformation will be brought about in our time simply by following the adage: "If you can't lick 'em, join 'em":

> The church will not regain its vitality—if that is to happen—by simply being hipper than thou. It must, to be sure, fight for the earthly implication of the heavenly values it affirms; it can never again divorce God from the Negroes, the poor, those dying in war, and the rest of humanity. But over and above that witness to the temporal meetings of the eternal, there must be the assertion of the eternal itself. And, amid all the showmanship and swinging theology, this is what I miss.[5]

But, just as in periods of human confidence and exuberance we must be on guard against shallow optimism, so in periods when the theological task appears enormous and the tides are running the other way, we ought to resist the temptation to project our own confusion on the cosmos. The current death throes of theology do not indicate the death of God.

I am no stranger to the struggle for belief; and I do not mind sharing some of that struggle, if only it will be of some help to the young who frequently imagine that the middle-aged have "arrived" at some comfortable plateau. While I am not nearly so intense about problems of belief as I once was, I am still very much in transit. I lay no claim to being a theologian, but I suspect that others of my age will recall grappling some years ago with some of the very problems now being articulated under the banner of newness. My files have quite a few notes and jottings (mostly to myself, though occasionally in sermons) made during the early fifties. Let me share just a few:

> Clearly, the world view of the Bible is no longer our world view. We do not believe in a three-decker universe. But how make sense of the ascension and the resurrection without it—or most of the Apostles' Creed? If we demythologize, that is, reinterpret biblical accounts in modern thought forms, what is left seems only tangentially Christian. What can a twentieth-century man make of the declaration that a man rose from the grave? On the other hand, what can one really make of Christianity without it?

> Christianity claims that its committed are freed by Christ's spirit from the gods of this world. Yet, in all honesty, can I affirm that the people I know in the churches, including the most committed, including the pastors (and myself!), seem any more free than the general run of men? Does it not appear that we are more determined by genetic chance and the psychological *milieu* of childhood than by any subsequent confession of faith? Don't Christians presume and claim too much, much too much?

> How often it seems to me, in making pastoral calls, that religion does indeed operate in the way the Freudians claim, as a barrier to maturity. In how many of the people I visit does religion seem to function as childish illusion rather than strengthening preparation for service? How disappointing it is to meet an otherwise intelligent man and discover that his religion appears to be a kind of insurance policy—or a way of guaranteeing his position in life. And how little connection there appears to be between the people who love the old hymns and commune faithfully and any concern for social justice and civil rights!

> Looking back over the years, I realize how much I have changed since college days. Then, possibly as part

of my identity search, I was much concerned with prayer and longed for a sense of oneness with the universe, with God. Prayer was very important to me. Now that I am a minister, isn't it ironic that prayer, in any vital sense, seems to have ebbed? It is not that I feel hypocritical about my public prayers; I try to keep them honest. It's that I am increasingly conscious of the extent to which, operationally, the personal God seems to have been dying within. Without any conscious recognition of it, I seem to operate mostly as other men do, on the evidence of my senses. If there is such a thing as a fully secular man, I wonder what difference there would be between my way of operating and his.

My jottings today would differ somewhat. I include those above only as a sample of the kinds of questions which, in my experience, have been troubling people within the churches for some time.

My own response to the theologians in question is not, then, concern about their attacks on "orthodoxy." It is just that I do not find in their writings much of an alternative to my central dilemmas. I miss in them a balanced attention both to the current scene and to the richness of the Christian tradition. I miss in them what I can only term the dimensions I discern in the Niebuhrs and Tillich. And I cannot join them in celebrating the secular world as an unmixed blessing.

Does not the much-heralded theological "new optimism" of several years ago now have a hollow sound in the wake of the civil rights movement and the Vietnamese tragedy? Is it an accident that we are now discussing hope? Is there not a disturbing parallel between the anti-institutionalism of recent theology and the near-anarchic assumption of young militants, white and black, that no possibilities remain for working through established processes of government? Are we to stop speaking of "transcendence" because current philosophical streams flow elsewhere? Is it true that belief in God is the enemy of human freedom . . . Jesus' belief, too? If "God talk" is not acceptable, how about all the "Jesus talk"? And, if God is really dead, then has not death become God, Death the ultimate definer of all things, the definer of our hopes and dreams?

My own belief is that it is still possible to locate oneself somewhere within the tradition, indeed that the tradition contains that basic conviction without which life itself may seem a living death. I suspect I am reaffirmed in this conviction by my interest in contemporary literature. Listen, for example, to the perceptive words of John W. Hunt in *William Faulkner: Art in Theological Tension:* "The extremity of man's condition in Faulkner—in a Quentin or a Hightower, a Christmas . . . is not simply that God is dead while man is still intact and able to function meaningfully. Rather it is that in all meaningful ways man is dead too. *God's death means the death of man.*" H. Richard Niebuhr's words also find me: "To deny the reality of a supernatural being called God is one thing; to live without confidence in some center of value and without loyalty to a cause is another."[6]

The philosopher William James once lectured to a huge audience on the probable origins of the universe. At his conclusion, an old lady asked: "On what is the universe founded?" Admitting that he had no certain answer, James asked for his questioner's opinion. "Why, on a rock!" said she. "Well then," he said, "on what is the rock founded?" "On another rock." "And *that* rock?" Drawing herself up stiffly, the tenacious one settled the matter: "Young man, get one thing straight. With me it's rocks all the way."

While we may not like that lady's dogmatism, we've got to admire her spirit. And I suggest that it is one of man's perennial needs, by no means lessened in our day, to find something dependable on which to base his life. All men need something in which to believe, and if they do not articulate it and confess it openly, it does not mean that covert convictions do not operate slyly behind the scenes.

With regard to Christian faith, it would seem to me that those in quest of something solid will be aided by requiring at least three things of their developing *credo:* that it be *relevant* in our world; that, in addition, it be *open,* not only to the future, but to the spirit and substance of biblical faith; and that, in order clearly to understand how we agree and differ with others, it offer something *distinctive* in the face of our common human dilemma. Relevance, openness, distinctiveness: three marks of a maturing belief.

All faith involves risk, and brief statements of faith involve the risk of oversimplification. Nonetheless I suggest that the bedrock affirmation of the biblical tradition and the backbone of Christian theology is the courageous conviction: God is Love. This means, if I understand it correctly, that the ultimate nature of reality, the way things are, the mystery that underlies the miracles of birth and death, is concerned about and faithful to human beings. Think of it! At the heart of the universe: love!

The biblical affirmation, not to be sentimentalized or abstracted from other truths, expresses, in Reinhold Niebuhr's words, "a basic trust in the meaningfulness of human existence." Erik Erikson's study *Childhood and Society* discloses the key problem of the infant to be the achievement of a basic trust in life. Christian faith discloses the ongoing necessity of such trust as the lifeblood of the human enterprise. Put on Paul's lips, the affirmation swells to majestic heights: "I am convinced that there is nothing in death or life, in the realm of spirits or superhuman powers, in the world as it is or the world as it shall be, in the forces of the universe, in heights or depths—nothing in all creation that can separate us from the love of God in Christ Jesus our Lord" (Rom. 8:38–39, NEB).

Believable or incredible, good news or pious illusion, there is little question that this is a belief only too painfully relevant to our world. Leaving aside the legions of the unserious and indifferent, can we conceive a word that more clearly describes the nature of the twentieth-century quest for meaning than the word agony? Do men trust life in our era? Are they able to affirm anything beyond the passing parade of pain and pleasure, shadow and light, birth and death? Are not most of us contemporary Manichaeans, convinced that the world is in a death struggle between the forces of light and darkness, and compelled to check each day's headlines for the latest reports? Albert Camus, in his famous address to a group of Dominican monks, sounded a familiar note: "I share with you your abhorrence of evil. But I cannot share your hope. I refuse to believe in a god who allows the suffering of innocent children."

I have no confident reply to that. Do you? Has not belief's central task always been to reconcile a loving God with the world's apparently senseless evil and suffering? When all the world's theodicies have had their say, and splendid have been the attempts, the mystery remains: Why? Why the unresolved agonies of men and women who long to believe, but in the face of the facts feel they cannot? The Bible, too, faithful portrayer of our humanity, knows countless days when the tortured question is wrung from the lips of the faithful—of Job, of the psalmist, of our Lord: "Why hast thou forsaken me?" (Matt. 27:46b)

To many observers the world looks more like a sinister plot than a creation of love. "That devil God!" cries Zorba the Greek. "There are times," writes Herman Melville, "in this strange mixed affair we call life when a man takes this whole universe for a vast practical joke."

But the joke isn't funny. James Gould Cozzens, in *By Love Possessed*, and Tennessee Williams, in play after play, suggest that at the heart of life lies horror. And the lonely old man in Hemingway's "A Clean, Well-Lighted Place" rephrases the Lord's Prayer: "Our nada [nothing] who are in nada, nada be thy name. . . ." For how many has the modern experience been one of despair? Is it not clear that however difficult it may be to affirm, however contrary to much of life as we see it, the affirmation of the love of God, like a surgeon's knife, cuts directly into the central agony of our time? Dorothy Sayers was quite correct: whatever else you may say about the Christian creeds, they are not boring. If they are correct, and they are claims to truth, they make all the difference in the world. This central belief speaks to our condition. It is clearly *relevant*.

Beyond that, it seems to me that the affirmation of the love of God is a direct link to most of what is central in the long tradition of Jew and Christian through the ages. It is a belief open both to past and future. It is a responsible word. Nathaniel Hawthorne, in *The Blithedale Romance*, refers with some irony to some old men who "kept a death grip on one or two ideas which have not come into vogue since yesterday morning." We are dealing with just such an idea.

An absurd notion in the modern world? Think what it must have seemed to the ancient Jews. On the face of it, nothing would seem more contrary to their experience. As Carlyle Marney has it, in *The Recovery of the Person*, they were:

> an unhappy and jealous association of wild desert nomads, caught between the crushing power of the three mightiest empires of the ancient world. They were constantly being overrun by armies, or fighting among themselves. They were victims of captivity, leprosy, treachery, idolatry, and the invasion of other cults and cultures. Their best king was a model of murder, deceit, and chicanery. Their best prophets were stoned, sawed asunder, or made prisoners for life. Their best temple was an unrecognizable pile of rubble throughout most of its history. Their best poetry was about a God who led them into captivity. . . . Their best ethic produced a crowd of Pharisees . . . ; their best law was an unkeepable demand.[7]

Do you see how remarkable a thing it is that out of this context comes an irrepressible belief in the love of God?

> Hear, O Israel: the Lord our God is one Lord; and thou shalt love the Lord thy God with all thine heart.

After Dachau and Auschwitz, which by any simple reckoning ought to silence faith forever, the word persists:

> Give thanks to him, bless his name!
> For the Lord is good;
>   his steadfast love endures forever,
>   and his faithfulness to all generations.

Those early Christians too. They would not have been big buyers of *The Power of Positive Thinking*. "We are handicapped," wrote Paul, "on all sides, but we are never frustrated; we are puzzled but never in despair. We are persecuted, but we never have to stand it alone: we may be knocked down but we are never knocked out!" (2 Cor. 4:8–9, Phillips)

What apparently sustained them was the belief that what had happened in Jesus, their lord, was living proof that man never need walk alone; that isolation is not the last word; that death is not the last word; that guilt is not the last word; that the last word on everything was the love of God, now shown clearly to them in Jesus, who had lived among them.

"You may be confused by the issues of life," writes Harold Blake Walker, "haunted by its frustrations, baffled by its circumstances. But you are never lost if you are loved." Isn't this true to our experience? Whatever the despair or hurt, whatever the heartache, doesn't it tend to be resolved in the presence of those we love? Does the child, frightened as much as hurt by his fall, receive more from the iodine or from the comforting arms? Does the emotionally disturbed person benefit more from psychiatric theory or from the trained capacity of his therapist to practice genuine acceptance?

Jesus looked at the facts of life and flung the word Father into the cosmos. The word, I'm told, is actually closer to our "daddy," a circumstance most disturbing to the Pharisees. Is he to be trusted? Does his vision hold? "I am persuaded," said the apostle, "that nothing can separate us from the love of God. . . ." This central affirmation speaks to our world and is creatively open to past and future.

Now, finally, is there anything *distinctive* in it, does it offer something not usually found in the rival "faiths" on campus? I submit that it does, and do not mean thereby a slur on other points of view. I mean simply that I don't know where else to go for a foothold which seems adequate on the slippery terrain of this world. I suppose my need is that of Melville's Captain Ahab: "I like a good grip; I like to feel something in this slippery world that can hold, man!" Faith or illusion, reality or phantom, the affirmation serves the life and sustains the spirit.

I don't find any foothold in the many varieties of humanism that are among us, though I am deeply sympathetic to much that humanists believe and am more fellow traveler with them than with most who bear the label "religious." But I am convinced that any really effective basis for the human values we share needs more than a human referent. I do not choose to argue with those who testify otherwise. I rest my case: for me, humanism is a dead-end street.

Nor do I find any final foothold in what has become for many the last bastion of defense: human love. I would be among the last to discount its crucial importance; our lives are made or broken by the quality of human relationships. Indeed, so wonderful is human love that religion borrows its basic imagery from the family. God is like a father. All men are brothers. But can the human spirit survive the deserts of cosmic aloneness?

> Blow on the coal of the heart.
> The candles in churches are out.
> The lights have gone out in the sky.
> Blow on the coal of the heart
> > And we'll see by and by . . .

> —Archibald MacLeish[8]

Modest enough, this, but hardly an answer to the thirsty spirit. Robert Penn Warren, in his perspective introduction to Hemingway's *A Farewell to Arms*, writes that it is in a world where people experience life as ultimately meaningless that the cult of love develops.

So, standing on the shore of the sea in an age when science seemed to have killed religion, Matthew Arnold penned his haunting "Dover Beach":

> Ah, love, let us be true
> To one another! for the world, . . .
> . . . .
> Hath really neither joy, nor love, nor light,
> . . . .
> And we are here as on a darkling plain
> Swept with confused alarms of struggle and
> > flight,
> Where ignorant armies clash by night.

But human love, the loveliest thing this side of eternity, contains no guarantees. All this becomes painfully clear at the end of Hemingway's *A Farewell to Arms*. Catherine Barkley is dead. Frederick returns to the hospital room for a last visit: "It wasn't any good. It was like saying good-bye to a statue. After a while I went out and left the hospital and walked back to the hotel in the rain." What man loves always vanishes. Unless there is more than this, is any kind of trust possible?

How about nature? There is health, in our speeded-up, pressurized society, in liberal doses of communion with mother earth. But the natural world does not provide much of a bulwark against despair. Nature, "the great mother of us all," heals but also kills us, gives us solace but also erupts in fury. Show a child a snake swallowing a tiny creature and then urge him to trust nature. Watch a hawk capture a rabbit and see if you learn here about a God of love. Consider the countless millions killed in human history by caprice of fire, flood, disease, and famine, the ravages of nature which have laid low more even than man's fiendish devices. Trust nature? Nature's out to get us!

But, if nature yields no solid ground for faith, why can't we rest our case on the drama of mankind itself, the fascinating pageant of human history? Certainly we do well to learn from history. Thomas Babington Maccaulay once said: "Those who compare the age in which their lot has fallen with a golden age which exists only in imagination may talk of degeneracy and decay; but no man who is correctly informed as to the past will be disposed to take a morose or desponding view of the present."

Yet while these observations well remind us not to exaggerate present problems, they also remind us that the human condition has always been a torn and tenuous affair. I would like to believe William Faulkner when he speaks, in his University of Virginia lectures, of "man's fine record." But I have read Faulkner's novels and have seen where his vision leads; the history of Yoknapatawpha County is the history of our world, sprinkled with nobility and courage but also deeply stained with greed, selfishness, and violence. He who would scan history for comfort must reckon with Calvary, Buchenwald, and the slums of Harlem, if he would see steadily and whole. And as for inevitable progress, do any still believe? Isn't it increasingly

DON HERZBACH

clear that as our human possibilities unfold before us, our potential evil and destructiveness keeps pace? Do the decades ahead mean the promised land—or 1984?

Whatever lies ahead quite clearly will require a special toughness and resilience; whatever the future holds will demand persistent commitment, the willingness to work patiently and courageously to improve our world, to see to it that our most cherished values are not swallowed up by advancing technology. And to maintain that toughness and resilience, that patience and commitment, will take an act of faith.

I mean by faith not centrally assent to one or another doctrine, though what one believes is clearly crucial. Nor do I mean "believing what you know ain't so" or taking refuge in the "spiritual." I mean by faith an act of intellectual courage, a refusal to be overcome by the stubborn contradictions of life. I mean a willingness to stretch one's mind beyond the safe and tested in continuing quest of wholeness. I mean the willingness to dream, to plan, to maintain fidelity to the human adventure.

I confess that I can locate no other credible basis for such faith than that which has been given to us: the conviction that the human drama is not self-containing, but is part of a larger one; that we are loved and confirmed as personal centers of being by Him in whom we have been given life; and that, finally, even our botching of the whole human enterprise, as horrible as that prospect is, will not detract from His loving purposes.

I am well aware that such a conviction cannot be proved; one trusts or one does not. In my own struggle, I have been greatly helped by words of H. Richard Niebuhr in *Radical Monotheism and Western Culture:*

> By whatever name we call it, this law of things, this reality, this way things are, it is something with which we all must reckon. We may not be able to give a name to it, call it only the "void" out of which everything comes and to which everything returns. But it is there . . . the last shadowy and vague reality, the secret of existence by virtue of which things come into being and by virtue of which they pass away.

Now a strange thing has happened in our history and in our personal life: our faith has been attached to that great void, to that enemy of all our causes, to that opponent of all our gods. We have been enabled to say of it, "Though it slay us, yet will we trust it."

Niebuhr adds: "The fact remains that when this faith was given, Jesus Christ was there."[9] The resurrection, however it is given one to understand it, is surely the supreme symbol of affirmation, the daring proclamation of the victory of life over the powers of darkness.

For me, the key question is not the existence of God or his alleged death; the key question is the nature of that reality which ultimately undergirds and supports this whirling ball of mud and all that's on it. To trust that the nature of that reality has been most clearly disclosed to us in Jesus is about as close as I can get to summing up.

I'm sure the terrain I occupy will seem barren to some. I can understand why, and I am often struck by my own audacity at speaking and writing to other men about God. But whatever affirming I'm able to do isn't mine anyway. I can only point to it: "Neither death, nor life . . . nor anything else in all creation will be able to separate us from the love of God in Christ Jesus our Lord."

Anyhow, I spent most of my junior
and senior years at a bar downtown
chugging drafties and forgetting
I was going nowhere. It's hard to
explain. I wanted to be motivated.
I wanted something to reach out
and turn me on, but there was
nothing there.
>   —a graduate

Listen! I will be honest with you.
I do not offer you the old
  smooth prizes,
but offer you new, rough prizes.
>   —Walt Whitman

The illusion that times that *were*
are better than times that *are*
has probably pervaded all ages.
>   —Horace Greeley

There are those who maintain that
the situation is too grave for us
to do much about it.... It is good
that Moses did not study
theology under the teachers
of that message.... Otherwise,
I would still be in Egypt,
building pyramids.
>   —Abraham Joshua Heschel[1]

11

TOWARD COMMIT-MENT

The book of Ecclesiastes was written more than twenty centuries ago, but I suspect today's students will find its mood strikingly contemporary. It is a timely reminder that we ignore history only at the risk of ignorance. The writer, whom we call Koheleth, had a vigorous mind. A man with a passion for life, he tried everything, and ended up disillusioned: "Vanity of vanities! All is vanity" (1:2b). As for academic pursuits, his conclusion was a familiar one to all who had burned the midnight oil: "Of making many books there is no end, and much study is a weariness of the flesh" (12:12b). The pursuit of knowledge? "He who increases knowledge increases sorrow" (1:18b). Koheleth apparently worked pretty hard at the pursuit of pleasure and material gain, only to conclude that here, too, "all was vanity and a striving after wind" (2:11). His critique of society is just as bitter. Injustice and poverty continue to plague the world, many of those in high office misuse their authority and, he concludes in familiar words, "money answers everything" (10:19b). Try as he might to avoid it, Koheleth's observations lead him to a cynical hedonism: "Let a man eat, drink, and be merry, for tomorrow he dies."

When all is said and done, higher education will have

failed today's students if they lack either a clear-eyed picture of our world or the desire to work to improve it. Like ancient Koheleth, we live in a world which constantly threatens to overwhelm us with disillusionment and cynicism. It is a world in which personal security seems ever more difficult, as men are caught in the pattern of relentless social change. It is a world seemingly in the grip of the technological furies, in which few appear to ask whether a new bomb, a new tail fin, or a new moon shot will enhance or imperil life on this earth. It is a world in which talk of peace continues unabated while in the wings hovers the specter of global destruction, a world in which those wounded by new-style warfare are healed with smooth and humane proficiency while the wounding and the warring go on. At our fingertips are the means for international communciation, shrinking the earth; in our hearts, simple communication among people and cultures remains inhibited. The nation-state and war itself linger on, grimly reminding us that "man come of age" has yet to learn to live with his fellowmen.

But it *is* our world. And describing it is not nearly enough. Whatever vocational choices today's students make, there has likely never been a time which more called for the needed combination of brains, guts, and integrity. Nor, I think, have we ever needed more the reaffirmation of the stuff of human life, what William Faulkner once called "the old verities and truths of the heart, the old universal truths, lacking which any story is ephemeral and doomed, love and honor and pity and pride and compassion and sacrifice."

As is often the case, a poet captures the heart of a thing best; and as a metaphor for responsible commitment in today's world, we can do worse than Robert Frost's "The Lesson for Today":

> And were an epitaph to be my story
> I'd have a short one ready for my own.
> I would have written of me on my stone:
> I had a lover's quarrel with the world.[2]

That arresting phrase, "a lover's quarrel with the world," strikes me as a creative response to our contemporary Koheleths, the voices of cynicism and despair. At the heart both of the prophetic biblical tradition and of the liberal arts education is a summons to men and women to quarrel seriously with the prevailing culture. But the quarrel is conditioned; it is to spring from affection and regard, a lover's quarrel with the world.

Students and colleges have failed each other, I think, if students do not leave campus determined to keep alive the kind of questions and concerns which have faced them during the undergraduate years. If college has not meant the widening of experience, the transformation of mind and heart, the determination to use energies and abilities where they are needed, then education has been nipped in embryo. It will be all too easy for young people to become "acculturated" and, instead of rocking boats, simply row them down one or another stream. Plain old selfishness remains a popular life-style. Can colleges expect more than that? Can they dare hope that some have picked up in their bustling halls and classrooms profound biases toward humane and responsible living?

I am well aware that words like honor and sacrifice and commitment do not come easily to this generation. It does not like to wear its concern on its sleeve and I, for one, have great respect for that. But the fact remains that unless colleges *pass* on the culture as well as pass *on* the culture, they have done a half-job. No college worth the name should regard itself simply as a transmission belt for the conventional wisdom, nor should it set out merely to serve society's goals, particularly when the goals themselves may need rethinking.

We are therefore urged to quarrel with this world, confused and messed up as it is, to search out its cores of injustice, its places of moral dry rot, its wastelands of the tawdry and trivial. We are asked to keep challenging that which is phony and senseless. Nor are we to repeat the fatal error of confusing adulthood with mere conformity. There is much that needs changing.

Every generation, I suppose, regards its inheritance as a particularly odious thing. I know how persistent are the pressures and uncertainties of our world. It may help us somewhat to remember that today's parents, many of them, were also less than enthusiastic about things as they found them. Many of them left school, jobs, and loved ones and went through the wrenching experience of a terrible war, and have since lived through years of uneasy peace and ceaseless change. I suppose no generation has ever had an easy time of it.

But that doesn't erase the dilemmas; nor are they eased by the accelerating confusion of roles and values in our culture, making normally difficult decisions ever harder. Herman Melville wrote in *Mardi:* "The guidebook that served the father cannot serve the son." It is true that some of the old rules don't fit the new game, and also that we continue to face uncertainties in matters of morality and religion and the quest for meaning. But one hopes that today's students have discovered some things in their heritage which are worth preserving. And that they keep in mind that Elijah's ancient lament has been the sad self-discovery of many a generation come of age: "Now, O Lord, take away my life; for I am no better than my fathers" (1 Kings 19:4b).

During the college years, the more sensitive and concerned have shown a good deal of discontent. They have rightly been bothered by continued discrimination against black Americans. They have asked why poverty and squalor must continue in an otherwise affluent society, and have dared to suggest that the world's real enemy may be, not creeping communism, but gnawing hunger. They have asked, as maturing citizens of this country, disturbing questions about our foreign policy—in particular, about our involvement in Vietnam. And they have raised questions about the quality of life in these United States. *Time's* 1966 "man of the year," that contemporary Koheleth from California, bristled with indignation:

> Look at you, brainwashing a whole generation of kids into getting a revolving charge account and buying your junk. (Who's a junkie?) Look at you, needing a couple of stiff drinks before you have the guts to talk with another human being. Look at you, making it with your neighbor's wife just to prove that you're really alive. Look at you, screwing up the land and the water and the air for profit and calling this nowhere scene the Great Society! C'mon, man, you've got to be kidding![3]

Some have begun to quarrel, in ways that look promising. But let's not pretend that the coals of concern and compassion

glow brightly in all. Some students have preferred and doubtless will continue to prefer the easier road of accommodation
and adjustment. Recall the frustration of the committed
teacher, pictured by poet W. D. Snodgrass in his little "Campus
on the Hill":

> What shall I say to the young on such a morning?—
>
> . . . .
> My little ones lean not toward revolt. They
> Are the Whites, the vaguely furiously driven, who resist
> Their souls with such passivity
> As would make Quakers swear. All day, dear Lord, all day
> They wear their godhead lightly.
> They look out from their hill and say,
> To themselves, "We have nowhere to go but down;
> The great destination is to stay."[4]

The great destination is to stay! What a damning indictment
of all who move too smoothly into our highly organized society, who adjust quickly to injustice, look out for "number
one," learn the language and ethos of game-playing and rise to
positions of some importance, having gained their portion, but
at the price of their own integrity.

In 1789, Gouverneur Morris wrote to George Washington
about Louis XVI: "He is a good man. In ordinary times he
would have made a good king. But he has inherited a revolution." We, too, have inherited a revolution, a world in which
private dreams and self-centered strategies will be irrelevant
and self-defeating. This may or may not be "the fun generation," but I suspect that the logic of life hasn't changed all
that much, and that those whose goals are mainly private and
whose commitment is to nothing larger than what William
James called "the convulsive little ego" are on their way to
emptiness. A generation ago, T. S. Eliot gave us a sobering
image of

> decent, godless people:
> Their only monument the asphalt road
> And a thousand lost golf balls.[5]

Update that, if you will, with "the pursuit of pleasure and a
thousand lost ideals," and listen once again to words from the

tradition of responsibility, words of Amos: "Take away from me the noise of your songs; to the melody of your harps I will not listen. But let justice roll down like waters, and righteousness like an everflowing stream" (5:23–24). And Micah: "He has showed you, O man, what is good; and what does the Lord require of you but to do justice, and to love kindness, and to walk humbly with your God?" (6:8) And Paul: "Do not be conformed to this world" (Rom. 12:2a).

Isn't it clear that not to quarrel with this world is really not to care about it? Some years ago, William Butler Yeats expressed the modern dilemma in a way that still rings true: "The best lack all conviction, while the worst/Are full of passionate intensity."[6] We should know by now that knowledge is not enough. For if the people with the brains don't have the love, the concern, what hope is there? If a man desires nothing more than to live comfortably, is he fully a man? The apostle Paul takes great pains, in the familiar chapter in 1 Corinthians, to make clear that unless learning is supplemented by love it means very little.

Now the second part of Frost's line: let our quarrel be a "lover's quarrel." It is one thing to quarrel; it is another to do so out of a deep regard and affection. One of Jim Crane's pointed cartoons comes to mind, showing a little fellow with a pair of scissors. Caption: "I don't make anything, but I'm a very good critic." Our world is full of critics; it has all too few people who know how to quarrel creatively.

Koheleth, the writer of Ecclesiastes, speaks not as one who loves his world but as one who cynically despairs of it. The authentic prophet loves his world even as he denounces it. Moses pleads with Jahweh on behalf of his people. Jesus weeps over Jerusalem. Martin Luther King prays for the souls of the white men who have kept his people in bondage. This world kills its prophets, but their protest has not been in vain.

Those among us who deny the voice of dissent on the grounds that it implies lack of patriotism or atheistic unconcern understand neither biblical religion nor responsible love of country. John Osborne, in *Look Back in Anger*, was much closer to truth: "To be angry is to care." America may be criticized out of love for America. Of course, there is a cheap kind of protest which costs little and which is rooted more in immaturity than in genuine concern. The mere label "dissenter" does not qualify one for a serious hearing, any more than angry protest is a substitute for careful thought and difficult reform. What has been most disheartening during the last few years has been not the demonstrations and protests, many of which have reflected genuine concern; what is dismaying is the apparently growing number of young people who do not care enough to remain angry. I speak of those who reject not only selected, visible aspects of our way of life, but who choose instead total rejection, alienation, disaffiliation. If enough of America's "angry young men," black and white, give up on America, then what hope America?

Kenneth Keniston's important study of a group of undergraduates, called *The Uncommitted*, gives us a close look at those Harvard students who represent the extreme of alienation, those at the opposite end of the spectrum from conformist, organizational types. Reminding us that the language of social commentary in our day is flooded with terms that show a growing distance between men and society, Keniston describes his subjects. They are pleasure-oriented and nihilistic in world view. Their quests are private quests—for sensation, for kicks and stimulation, sometimes for individual artistic expression. They have no interest in improving the world. Said one: "The modern world is going to hell, but since the race is doomed to die some day, I can't see that it makes much difference." Another: "I have come to experience horror at the good American way of life, the comfortable, middle-class existence. . . . This seems boring to me." The possibility that they themselves might be instruments of social change is rejected: "I leave speculation about world affairs to our politicians. . . . Political activity is like the games children play. . . . Whatever happens will not affect my thinking."[7] Rather than come to grips with an imperfect world, these young men prefer to create a better one inside their heads with drugs or fantasy.

If Keniston is correct, the most important aspect of his findings is that this extreme group has a great deal in common with many of their more conventional peers. What distinguishes today's rebels, says Keniston, from rebels of former generations is that the rebellion usually remains at the level of grumbling discontent.

A lover's quarrel with the world involves us in a great deal more than grumbling discontent. Not too long ago a series of fascinating essays, under the title *To Make a Difference*, turned up in the campus book shop. The pieces were written by a number of students at San Francisco State College, presumably those most vocal and articulate in their complaints. The *New York Times* reviewer, obviously over thirty, commented:

> When all is said, and resaid, these youngsters emerge as yet another generation that has discovered an imperfect world. They are against racial discrimination, poverty, the war in Vietnam. They think the American way of life is too comfortably material; they lament the loss of frontiers, of small towns, of innocence. What is new and disturbing here is the whining tone in which they deliver their accusations against their elders.[8]

Let yours be a lover's quarrel, involving continuing protest, but involving also deep caring for a troubled people. The difficult and often tedious work in politics, the renewing of the churches, entering into one's professional life with energy and integrity—all these involve courage and patience and some recognition of a claim superior to that of self, while the central temptation of the "intellectual" is to wax prophetic about the foibles of society over coffee, but steadfastly refuse to become involved in any of the structures within which change might be effected!

Remember that passage in *All Quiet on the Western Front*, in which a hospitalized soldier, to the amazement of his comrades, confesses to a misdemeanor of which he was innocent. "But why did you do that," they asked, "when it wasn't you at all?" The soldier laughed and told them, "It doesn't matter. You see, I got a lick on the head and they presented me with a certificate saying I was not responsible for my actions. Ever since then I've had a perfectly wonderful time."

It would not be difficult, at this point in history, for a man to plead psychic if not physical wounds, to settle for "a wonderful time," to let the rest of the world go by. The problem is complicated, since at this very moment when men need compassion and courage and conviction, many seem unable to draw sustenance from the ancient wells of inspiration and strength. It may be, indeed, that at this moment the only commitments one can honestly make are simple, human commitments. Let me say clearly that I know nothing in our common tradition which need discourage us from the centrality of these commitments. Experience may disclose, to be sure, that such commitments have a way of becoming thin and frazzled by the tensions and ambiguities of life unless they are supported by faith. There is at least a hint in Ecclesiastes that it is precisely apart from God that life trails off to futility. We may come to agree with Jacques Barzun that many of our troubles are "the troubles of men who, living at the raveled end of liberalism, have lost their religion and confused their obligations to one another." We may discover that the courage to live in this kind of a world requires a humble and healing relationship with life's source, a belief in God. We may come to see that what our society basically lacks is a vision of itself and of man that transcends technology, and that seeds of hope and sustenance for the human spirit lie in the very tradition we now reject, awaiting only the responsive heart in which to grow.

This world desperately needs intelligent people who will work to correct its injustices and evils. Griping is not nearly enough. Nor is cynical disavowal.

> The protest that matters is that which we manage to sustain . . . as our knowledge of the real world accumulates, and we suffer the painful process of reconciling ourselves to it. If, when we have learned that the walls of Jericho will not fall at the sound of a trumpet, that Jerusalem will not be built in a day, that Camelot in any age is a frail flower of chivalry—when we have learned how strong are the forces of evil and inaction in the world— if then, we have still managed to sustain a spirit of protest, it will be worth attention, and it will educate and reform.[9]

What more can the world hope from today's young person than this: that when he has met the test of responsibility and been tried in the crucible of experience, it will be reported of him, "He had a lover's quarrel with the world."

NOTES

EPIGRAPH

1. From *Giles Goat-Boy*, by John Barth. Copyright © 1966, by John Barth. Reprinted by permission of Doubleday & Company, Inc.

PREFACE

1. Paul Goodman in *Never Trust a God over Thirty*, ed. Albert H. Friedlander. Copyright 1967 by McGraw-Hill. Used with permission of McGraw-Hill Book Company.
2. *Ibid.*

CHAPTER 1

1. T. S. Eliot, "Ash Wednesday," *Collected Poems, 1909–1962* (New York: Harcourt, Brace & World, 1963), p. 86.
2. Reprinted from *Childhood and Society*, Second Edition, Revised & Enlarged by Erik H. Erikson. By permission of W. W. Norton & Company, Inc. Copyright 1950, © 1963 by W. W. Norton & Company, Inc.
3. From "Mending Wall" from *Complete Poems of Robert Frost.* Copyright, 1930, 1939 by Holt, Rinehart and Winston, Inc. Copyright 1942, © 1958 by Robert Frost. Copyright © 1967 by Lesley Frost Ballantine. Reprinted by permission of Holt, Rinehart and Winston, Inc.
4. Dorothy Sayers, *The Mind of the Maker* (Cleveland, O.: World Publishing Co., 1956), pp. 127–30. Copyright 1941 Dorothy L. Sayers. Used by permission of A. Watkins, Inc.

CHAPTER 2

1. Rita Dershowitz in "The Dialogue Between the Generations," *Harper's*, Vol. 235, No. 1433 (October 1967), p. 46.
2. Quotation from *Peanuts* by Charles M. Schulz—© 1959, 1960 United Features Syndicate.
3. Gotthard Booth, "The Hippies' Quest for Reality" (unpublished speech presented at Franklin and Marshall College, March 10, 1968).

CHAPTER 3

1. Rita Dershowitz in "The Dialogue Between the Generations," *Harper's*, Vol. 235, No. 1433 (October 1967), p. 46.
2. Henry Fairlie, "How Is Youth to Be Served?" *The New Republic*, Vol. 156, No. 14 (April 8, 1967), pp. 12–13.
3. *Ibid.*, p. 12.

CHAPTER 4

1. Reprinted from *Childhood and Society*, Second Edition, Revised & Enlarged by Erik H. Erikson. By permission of W. W. Norton & Company, Inc. Copyright 1950, © 1963 by W. W. Norton & Company, Inc.
2. John Updike, "Pigeon Feathers," *Pigeon Feathers* (New York: Knopf, 1962), p. 135.
3. Quotation from *Peanuts* by Charles M. Schulz—© 1964, 1965 United Features Syndicate.
4. *Ibid.*
5. Nathan M. Pusey, *The Age of the Scholar* (Cambridge, Mass.: Belknap Press of Harvard University Press, 1963), pp. 81–82.
6. Updike, *op. cit.*, pp. 129–30.
7. Pusey, *op. cit.*, p. 200.
8. Reprinted from *Time-Life Books* Special Report, *The Young Americans* © 1967 Time Incorporated.
9. William Muehl, "Social Change: Reform or Revolution" (unpublished speech presented at Franklin and Marshall College, April 8, 1968).

CHAPTER 5

1. T. S. Eliot, "The Love Song of J. Alfred Prufrock," *Collected Poems, 1909–1962* (New York: Harcourt, Brace & World, 1963), p. 6.
2. *Ibid.*, "The Waste Land," p. 69.
3. By Tom Paxton, used by permission of Deep Fork Music, Ins. © 1964, 1965.
4. T. S. Eliot, *The Cocktail Party* (New York: Harcourt, Brace & Co. 1950), p. 134. Used by permission of Harcourt, Brace & World.
5. Eliot, "The Hollow Men," *op. cit.*, p. 79.

CHAPTER 6

1. Saul Bellow, *Herzog* (New York: Viking Press, 1964), p. 204.
2. Will Durant, quoted in "The Second Sexual Revolution," *Time*, Vol. 83, No. 4 (January 24, 1964), p. 59.

3. Phyllis and Eberhard Kronhausen, *Sex Histories of American College Men* (New York: Ballantine Books, 1960), p. 223.
4. W. H. Auden, "A Christmas Oratorio," *For the Time Being* (New York: Random House, 1944), p. 111.

CHAPTER 7

1. From *Giles Goat-Boy*, by John Barth. Copyright © 1966, by John Barth. Reprinted by permission of Doubleday & Company, Inc.
2. *Ibid.*
3. John Gardener, "The College Experience Ahead" (unpublished speech presented at Rye, New York, March 2, 1965).

CHAPTER 8

1. From *A Treasury of Humorous Verse*, Black and Gold Library, Vol. 95. Used by permission of Liveright Publishers, New York.
2. Luigi Pirandello, "Six Characters in Search of an Author," *Naked Masks*, ed. Eric Bentley, English version by Edward Storer (New York: E. P. Dutton & Co., 1952), p. 265.
3. John Updike, "Lifeguard," *Pigeon Feathers* (New York: Knopf, 1962), p. 212.
4. Will Herberg, "Biblical Faith and Natural Religion," *Theology Today*, Vol. XI, No. 4 (January 1955), p. 466.

CHAPTER 9

1. T. S. Eliot, "The Waste Land," *Collected Poems, 1909–1962* (New York: Harcourt, Brace & World, 1963), p. 66.

CHAPTER 10

1. Paul Goodman in *Never Trust a God over Thirty*, ed. Albert H. Friedlander. Copyright 1967 by McGraw-Hill. Used with permission of McGraw-Hill Book Company.
2. Saul Bellow, *Herzog* (New York: Viking Press, 1964), p. 219.
3. Excerpt from the Princeton Weekly, June 7, 1963, as quoted by Dr. Wesley A. Hotchkiss in "To Grow Roots and Take Wings," The *Journal* of the Division of Higher Education, United Church for Homeland Ministries, Volume 2, No. 2, December, 1963. Reprinted with permission.
4. From *Giles Goat-Boy*, by John Barth. Copyright © 1966, by John Barth. Reprinted by permission of Doubleday & Company, Inc.
5. Michael Harrington, quoted by Schubert M. Ogden in "How Does God Function in Human Life?" *Christianity and Crisis*, XXVII, 8 (May 15, 1967), 105.
6. H. Richard Niebuhr, *Radical Monotheism and Western Culture* (New York: Harper & Row, 1960), p. 25.
7. Carlyle Marney, *The Recovery of the Person* (Nashville, Tenn.: Abingdon Press, 1961), p. 89.

130

8. Archibald MacLeish, *J. B.*, a Play in Verse (Boston: Houghton-Mifflin Co., 1961), p. 153.
9. Niebuhr, *op. cit.*, pp. 22, 20.

CHAPTER 11

1. Abraham Joshua Heschel, *The Insecurity of Freedom* (New York: Farrar, Straus & Giroux, 1966). Copyright © 1966 by Farrar, Straus & Giroux. Used by permission of Dr. Heschel and Farrar, Straus & Giroux.
2. From "The Lesson for Today" from *Complete Poems of Robert Frost.* Copyright 1930, 1939 by Holt, Rinehart and Winston, Inc. Copyright 1942, © 1958 by Robert Frost. Copyright © 1967 by Lesley Frost Ballantine. Reprinted by permission of Holt, Rinehart and Winston, Inc.
3. "The Inheritor," *Time*, Vol. 89, No. 1 (January 6, 1967), p. 20.
4. W. D. Snodgrass, "Campus on the Hill," *Heart's Needle* (New York: Knopf, 1959), pp. 34–35.
5. T. S. Eliot, "Choruses from 'The Rock,'" *Collected Poems, 1909–1962* (New York: Harcourt, Brace & World, 1963), p. 156.
6. W. B. Yeats, "The Second Coming," *Collected Poems* (New York: Macmillan, 1933). Copyright, 1950 by The Macmillan Company.
7. Kenneth Keniston, *The Uncommitted* (New York: Harcourt, Brace & World, 1965), pp. 57–58.
8. © 1967 by The New York Times Company. Reprinted by permission.
9. Henry Fairlie, "How Is Youth to Be Served?" *The New Republic*, Vol. 156, No. 14 (April 8, 1967), p. 14.